Cambridge Elements

Elements in the Philosophy of Immanuel Kant
edited by
Desmond Hogan
Princeton University
Howard Williams
University of Cardiff
Allen Wood
Indiana University

KANT INCORPORATED

Garrath Williams
Lancaster University

Shaftesbury Road, Cambridge CB2 8EA, United Kingdom

One Liberty Plaza, 20th Floor, New York, NY 10006, USA

477 Williamstown Road, Port Melbourne, VIC 3207, Australia

314–321, 3rd Floor, Plot 3, Splendor Forum, Jasola District Centre, New Delhi – 110025, India

103 Penang Road, #05–06/07, Visioncrest Commercial, Singapore 238467

Cambridge University Press is part of Cambridge University Press & Assessment, a department of the University of Cambridge.

We share the University's mission to contribute to society through the pursuit of education, learning and research at the highest international levels of excellence.

www.cambridge.org
Information on this title: www.cambridge.org/9781009641371

DOI: 10.1017/9781009641364

© Garrath Williams 2025

This publication is in copyright. Subject to statutory exception and to the provisions of relevant collective licensing agreements, with the exception of the Creative Commons version the link for which is provided below, no reproduction of any part may take place without the written permission of Cambridge University Press & Assessment.

An online version of this work is published at doi.org/10.1017/9781009641364 under a Creative Commons Open Access license CC-BY-NC 4.0 which permits re-use, distribution and reproduction in any medium for non-commercial purposes providing appropriate credit to the original work is given and any changes made are indicated. To view a copy of this license visit https://creativecommons.org/licenses/by-nc/4.0

When citing this work, please include a reference to the DOI 10.1017/9781009641364

First published 2025

A catalogue record for this publication is available from the British Library

ISBN 978-1-009-64137-1 Hardback
ISBN 978-1-009-64138-8 Paperback
ISSN 2397-9461 (online)
ISSN 2514-3824 (print)

Cambridge University Press & Assessment has no responsibility for the persistence or accuracy of URLs for external or third-party internet websites referred to in this publication and does not guarantee that any content on such websites is, or will remain, accurate or appropriate.

For EU product safety concerns, contact us at Calle de José Abascal, 56, 1°, 28003 Madrid, Spain, or email eugpsr@cambridge.org

Kant Incorporated

Elements in the Philosophy of Immanuel Kant

DOI: 10.1017/9781009641364
First published online: October 2025

Garrath Williams
Lancaster University
Author for correspondence: Garrath Williams, g.d.williams@lancaster.ac.uk

Abstract: Corporations are legal bodies with duties and powers distinct from those of individual people. Kant discusses them in many places. He endorses universities and churches; he criticises feudal orders and some charitable foundations; he condemns early business corporations' overseas activities. This Element argues that Kant's practical philosophy offers a systematic basis for understanding these bodies. Corporations bridge the central distinctions of his practical philosophy: ethics versus right, public versus private right. Corporations can extend freedom, structure moral activity, and aid progress towards more rightful conditions. Kant's thought also highlights a fundamental threat. In every corporation, some people exercise the corporation's legal powers, without the same liabilities as private individuals. This threatens Kant's principle of innate equality: no citizen should have greater legal rights than any other. This Element explores the justifications and safeguards needed to deal with this threat. This title is also available as Open Access on Cambridge Core.

This Element also has a video abstract:
www.cambridge.org/EPIK_Williams_abstract

Keywords: corporations, legal personality, innate equality, private right, public right

© Garrath Williams 2025

ISBNs: 9781009641371 (HB), 9781009641388 (PB), 9781009641364 (OC)
ISSNs: 2397-9461 (online), 2514-3824 (print)

Contents

1	Introduction	1
2	Corporations: Between Private and Public Right	8
3	Justifications and Safeguards	30
4	Incorporating Business	49
5	Conclusion: Kant Incorporated	71
	Kantian Texts and Abbreviations	75
	References	76

1 Introduction

1.1 What Is a Corporation?

Political parties, churches, businesses, charities, universities, trade unions: across the world, these organisations are usually *corporations*. They are central to every sphere of life, not just commerce. No one can doubt their importance.

This list also shows the diversity of corporations. Do they really come under the same concept? This Element argues that the same form underlies them all. It also shows why this form has proved so adaptable and so essential to complex, interconnected societies.

What is the underlying form? The word offers a first clue. 'To incorporate' is to form several things into one body. The word comes from Latin: *corpus* is a body. Compare the English 'corpse': a dead body.

Corporations are active bodies. They are artificial – deliberately formed out of several things: at least one person, usually some property. They are alive in the metaphorical sense that they are able to act. They can also die. For example, they may go bankrupt – a corporation must be able to pay its bills.

How can people and things make up a single 'body' with the power to act?

Science fiction has imagined techno-fixes. Like the Borg from *Star Trek*, perhaps human beings could become mere instruments of a single hive mind. Even if that is more fiction than science, it illustrates one thing. To act completely as one, people cannot act as if they have minds of their own. Human cooperation is vital, but we should be wary of the mindless mindset: 'just following orders'.

Philosophers often discuss collective action: wolves hunt as a pack, people walk together. Both instincts and intelligence may foster a 'meeting of minds'. But individual drives and desires can pull us apart. Freedom means collective action is usually temporary. If people have minds of their own, they may part company.

Lawyers tell us that a corporation exists 'only in contemplation of law' (*Trustees of Dartmouth College* 1819: 636). This cannot be the whole story – I have just noted the importance of people's involvement (§2.2). Still, I will argue that *law* unites those people, over and above any personal commitments or relationships or material factors. Legally, almost every organisation we know is a corporation, or sometimes, a network of corporations (§4.1.5).

1.2 Why Kant?

In my view, the basic distinctions of Kant's practical philosophy enable us to understand corporations. They illuminate the basic form. They show why the same form can have diverse manifestations. They show why corporations can be so valuable, and point to key dangers.

Kant discusses several types of corporation, including universities and churches and charitable foundations. Of course, he could hardly foresee the types of corporation which emerged after his death – political parties and businesses, for example. In any case, he did not address corporations in a systematic way – unlike Hegel, for example. (See the Appendix to Section 3.) Kant scholars have also ignored this topic. This Element aims to redress this.

For readers convinced of Kant's importance, let me stress the importance of this gap. Kant's approach is systematic: he insists that a metaphysics of morals must be complete (6:357). So Kantian theory is duty-bound to find a place for corporations: they are, after all, essential to modern societies.

I cannot show, here, that a Kantian approach is more insightful than others. My aim is more limited: to set out the account so that it can be evaluated – on its own merits and against alternatives.

Readers less sure of Kant's importance, or more doubtful of his systematic approach, might ask: Wouldn't it be better to turn to political theorists who consider corporations explicitly? Or since many types of corporation are quite recent, shouldn't we consider them on our own terms, rather than drawing on historical thinkers?

Perhaps. Still, most philosophers and political theorists have neglected corporations. (Levy 2014 discusses major exceptions.) Most contemporary political philosophy takes the existence of corporations for granted. Alternatively, it considers just one type, such as the business corporation. In my view, this leads us to downplay the importance of the corporate form itself. It also encourages us to miss its fundamental dangers.

1.3 Kant's 'Metaphysics of Morals'

In the *Groundwork to the Metaphysics of Morals* (1785), Kant analyses 'the moral law'. He offers several formulations of his famous Categorical Imperative – for example, '*So act that you use humanity, in your own person as well as in the person of any other, always at the same time as an end, never merely as a means*' (4:429, emphasis in original).

However, the *Groundwork* says almost nothing about law as an institution. Kant remarks that 'attacks on the freedom and property of others ... [make it] clear that the transgressor of the rights of human beings is disposed to *use* ... *others merely as a means*' (4:430, my emphasis). Otherwise, there are few clues that legal relations will be central to his last great work, *The Metaphysics of Morals* (1797).

Since corporations are legal entities, this Element mostly draws on the latter work. It also assumes some familiarity with Kant's main ideas there. (For an overview, see Ripstein 2010.) But I do want to briefly outline how Kant finally divides up 'morals' – the whole sphere of questions about how we should act, individually and collectively.

As noted, for Kant, metaphysics aspires to a complete system. Concepts must fit within a larger whole, dividing it completely. *The Metaphysics of Morals* has two parts: the *Metaphysical Foundations of the Doctrine of Right* and the *Metaphysical Foundations of the Doctrine of Virtue*.

'Right' is the sphere of law and political authority. The fundamental idea is that force is justified to uphold our freedom to act. Only legal institutions can do this rightfully. No one may be left out; everyone can be forced to submit to a legal system.

'Virtue' concerns how we should act; Kant's discussion usually assumes that our legal rights and duties are already in place. But virtue cannot be enforced; it represents the constraint that a person places upon themselves as they try to act well.

1.3.1 A Note on Words: Morality, Right, Ethics

Kant uses the following terms to cover questions of right and wrong: *Moralität, Sitten, Recht, Ethik, Tugend*. *Tugend* can be easily translated as 'virtue'. The other words cause more problems.

Moralität and *Sitten* were interchangeable for Kant. *Sitten* appears in the title of both the *Groundwork* and the *Metaphysics of Morals*. It is natural to use 'morality' or 'morals' for both.[1]

Kantians have settled on the word 'right' (singular) as a translation for *Recht*. This sounds more awkward than the older translation, 'justice'. But it reminds us that Kant's concerns do not map neatly onto modern debates: he is less concerned about the distribution of resources, for example. I will use 'right' and 'rightful' to mark Kant's concerns in the *Doctrine of Right*.

In everyday German, *Ethik* is not really distinct from *Moralität*. In the *Metaphysics of Morals*, however, Kant uses *Ethik* to express his concerns in the *Doctrine of Virtue*. Translating this as 'ethical' is obvious but tricky, since everyday English also uses 'ethics' and 'morality' interchangeably.

---

[1] There is a further tangle owing to Hegel and his translators. Criticising Kant's approach, Hegel distinguished *Moralität* and *Sitten*. His translators and commentators tend to use 'morality' and 'ethics' for these, respectively. Versions of this distinction have been influential in modern moral philosophy – for example, in Williams (1985).

In this Element, 'morality' or 'morals' refer to the wider concerns of practical philosophy. These combine questions of 'right' and 'virtue'. I mostly avoid 'ethics' and 'ethical', unless the context clearly points to questions of virtue.

1.3.2 The Basic Structure of Kantian Right

Kant's account of right is based on freedom. By this he means, 'being one's *own master*' or independence from other people's 'necessitating choice' (6:237 f). Freedom is an innate or 'inborn' (*angeboren*) right: it 'belongs to everyone by nature, independently of any juridical act' (6:237).

As Kant stresses, everyone has this right: each person's freedom must be compatible with the same freedom for others. Hence Kant also frames this right as 'innate *equality*: [each person's] independence from being bound by others to more than one can in turn bind them' (6:237).

If there were no such thing as right, 'necessitating' or 'binding' would only mean coercion. Chains or imprisonment bind someone, literally. Credible threats of violence may also necessitate. Kant uses 'bind' (*verbinden*) in a more restricted sense. Granted the idea of right, a person is 'bound' if someone else has rights concerning some aspect of their conduct. In a state of nature (that is, the absence of government), these rights are given only by reason. In normal circumstances, they are a matter of law: a legal system with coercive penalties binds everyone. (See also §4.4.2.)

When a legal system treats citizens as equally free, 'binding' becomes a decent, everyday matter. For example, if I refuse to lend you my umbrella, my decision binds you. This is not because I will use force or call the police, should you take it anyway: most likely, I will not. The point is that law recognises the umbrella as mine: my right to decide about it binds you and everyone else. In this case, the legal system is genuinely public: it binds us equally, to respect one another's rights and uphold equal freedom.

Our innate right to freedom provides the basis for all this: our rights and duties as private individuals; the state's duty to specify and enforce individual rights and duties, or more broadly, to uphold a public, rightful condition. Allow me to emphasise that freedom and equality are inseparable, for Kant. If someone has more power to bind me than I have to bind them, then I cannot act independently of their choices. Our inequality makes me unfree.

I will underline innate equality throughout this Element, because it has a radical implication. No corporation should ever be a mere means for people to pursue their private ends.

1.3.3 Kant's Distinctions between Private and Public, and the Idea of Civic Rights

The distinction between 'public' and 'private' plays a crucial role in this Element. But authors use these terms in many ways, and Kant himself moves between a more abstract and a more familiar usage.

In the Introduction to the *Doctrine of Right*, Kant distinguishes private and public right as the contrast between a state of nature and a civil condition. In the absence of government and law, there is only private right (6:242). By contrast, actual states create a public legal order. Then right is public (Capps & Rivers 2024: 1 f, 19).

This distinction reflects Kant's insistence that some rights require no public declaration (6:210). Our innate right to equal external freedom is axiomatic (6:267 f) – the basis of his whole theory. Kant then argues that it must be possible for people to 'acquire' further rights – to property and contract, for example. The form of these rights can be known by reason alone.

Reason also declares that people must enter a civil condition. Individual rights exist in the state of nature, but they are *merely* private; they are open to dispute and barely enforceable. A state of nature is therefore not rightful. We need states to uphold everyone's individual rights (see further §2.4.1).

In a civil condition, individual rights become 'public' in the abstract sense that they are legislated, adjudicated and enforced by the state (6:306). For example, everyone's individual property is 'public' in the sense that it is united 'under a general public possessor' (6:323) – that is, a legal system which upholds individual rights. Nonetheless, Kant also draws on a more familiar sense in which individual property is 'private' (6:323 f), in contrast to resources governed by the state.

The same ambiguity applies to contract. We usually think of contracts between individuals as 'private', and Kant himself sometimes speaks this way. In contrast to a contract between private persons, a treaty between states is a 'public contract' (6:342, 349). But even individual contracts are public in the sense that an injured party can go to a *public* court for redress – of course impossible in the state of nature.

This leaves Kant's readers with two versions of the public-private distinction. At the most abstract level, all right is 'private' in the state of nature and 'public' in a civil condition. However, this Element presupposes a public legal order. As I explore in §2.2, corporations are 'artificial legal persons': they cannot exist without law. I will therefore bracket the abstract distinction.

Instead, I emphasise the more familiar distinction. This contrasts the powers of public authorities and private individuals *within* a legal order.

Only a public state can legislate, adjudicate, and enforce penalties or compensation. Only a public authority can tax or organise public spaces such as roads or markets (6:325 ff). Only a public official can exercise state powers. By contrast, only a 'private person' (6:324) can exercise private rights such as property and contract, or pursue their own private purposes.

In what follows, then, 'public right' relates to states and their powers and officials (§2.4.1). 'Private' concerns individual people and their rights as private individuals.

One further complexity: in a civil condition, people are citizens. As *members of the public* (6:314 f), we have rights that can only be conceived in terms of a public legal order. I already mentioned one: the right to go to court to enforce a contract. A right to free movement requires public highways (§3.4.1). Subject to various conditions, a person may have a right to create a corporation or participate in one.

These rights cross the more familiar public-private distinction. When I use a road to move from one place to another, I act privately: my purposes are my own. If I use a road for political protest, I act publicly: my purposes are civic. There is an obvious sense in which free movement is a *private right*: public highways are regulated so that everyone can reach their individual destinations, independently of other people's plans and purposes. Political protest is obviously a public matter. I will call it a *civic right*, rather than a public one, since 'private citizens' may not exercise public powers directly – only public, state officials can do this.

Below, I argue that when someone founds a corporation – a charity, for example – they exercise a right that depends on public authorisation and must be justified in public terms. In the terms just given, they exercise a *civic* right.

One final note: Kant also speaks of the public and private *use of reason*. This distinction is quite different: see §3.2.3 and §4.4.4.

1.3.4 Public Right beyond Individual States

Kantian public right is global in form. Each state must uphold rights within its territory. Since there are many states, there are questions about how they should relate to one another – Kant calls this 'right of nations'. 'Cosmopolitan right' concerns relations between states and people from outside their borders.

In this Element, I set international aspects to one side. They are vital when it comes to transnational business corporations and some non-governmental organisations (such as Amnesty International or Oxfam). These are actually networks of corporations, with member corporations based in several states

(§4.1.5). I hope to consider international dimensions in future work, but here focus on the simpler case.

1.4 Corporations Bridge Kant's Stark Distinctions

Corporations are formed from categories on both sides of Kant's distinctions. They combine public authority and private initiative. They involve both right and virtue, exercising legal powers in ways that also require ethical judgement. These different aspects of morality are tightly entwined in our everyday lives.

Laws governing individuals are mainly negative: *thou shalt not* infringe on others' rights. In decent political conditions, states do not tell us how to lead our lives or what purposes to adopt.

For Kant, virtue guides us as we exercise these rights and freedoms. The *Doctrine of Virtue* teaches some qualities of character and warns against some vices. Its main positive guidance is to take other people's happiness as our end. This leads to 'imperfect' duties – for example, 'be a useful member of the world' (6:446).

Duties are never optional, but imperfect duties are open-ended. What should you do, to be 'a useful member of the world'? Much depends on your specific situation and character. Each person must choose 'what sort of life he would like to lead and whether he has the powers necessary for it (e.g. whether it should be a trade, commerce, or a learned profession)' (6:445).

As Kant suggests, existing social possibilities guide our decisions. For example, we choose between careers and organisations. Most of these possibilities involve corporations. In Kant's day, much trade was incorporated in guilds and regulated companies. Now, almost all commerce is corporate. The learned professions have been incorporated for a very long time – the University of Bologna has been a corporation for over 800 years.

These modes of cooperation also enable *reciprocity*. One way to use someone as a 'mere means' is to have them pursue your ends without recognition or reward. One way to make yourself a mere means is to allow other people to do this (the vice of servility: see §§3.3.1–2). Contract right enables people to make reciprocal arrangements: to act as means but not *mere means* for one another (Feyerabend 27:1319). But even in Kant's day, and even more in ours, we rarely negotiate one-to-one. Corporations structure and compensate many social contributions.

In decent social conditions, corporate roles guide rather than determine. We have opportunities to move between roles, to alter roles, even to organise things in new ways. Corporations set most terms and conditions, while providing ways to revise these. They provide structure and orientation, recognition and reward, opportunities for virtuous commitment and initiative. They are vital to our lives and our contributions to others' lives.

1.5 The Structure of This Element

Section 2 examines the corporate form in terms of Kant's division between private rights and public authority. Corporations represent a remarkable legal 'technology'. They bring people and resources together for specific purposes; they combine flexibility (including scope for individual and collective initiative) and stability (in terms of juridical structure and accountability).

Section 3 explores Kantian justifications for incorporation, and the safeguards it needs. On the basis that corporations exist between public and private right, I consider how Kantian public right and virtuous ends might justify corporations, before turning to a possible argument from rights to freedom. I also note reasons for caution. Corporations have legal powers to govern persons and resources. They can undermine public and private right, misdirect and misinform. They can corrupt people's moral sense and lead us into all sorts of corrupt activities.

Section 4 turns to the type of corporation that dominates our world: the business corporation. Kant only saw the beginnings of this development: state-sponsored monopolies like the Dutch and English East India companies. He could not foresee political decisions to allow people to create business corporations on their own initiative. This section is therefore more speculative. I ask what follows from the principles set out above, focusing on business corporations with directors, shareholders and employees. I suggest that Kantians should have serious reservations about this structure.

Section 5 is a brief conclusion. It emphasises three points. First, corporate activity involves a combination of 'autonomy' and 'heteronomy'. Second, I reflect on the central metaphor I use in this Element: corporations exist *between* private rights and public power. Third, when states authorise corporations, justification and accountability are crucial. This requires reliable, public mechanisms to create and share knowledge about their activities.

2 Corporations: Between Private and Public Right

Corporations bridge Kant's divisions in the *Doctrine of Right*.

Corporations do not arise from private right. Private rights concern individual people or relate a few named persons. Corporations may involve thousands of people. People may leave; others may join. Every corporation affects everyone's rightful situation, in ways that private right does not.

Corporations are distinct from the state: they have their own purposes and powers. They may contest state policies, like a political party in opposition. They may have purposes separate from the state, like a church.

This section shows how corporations exist between public and private right. They rely on state authority. But people govern them without direct state involvement; they depend on people's voluntary participation; sometimes, people can create corporations on their own initiative.

The result is organisations that stand at arm's length from the state. This is possible through four interrelated features, which I will explain below: legal personality, purpose, participation, and government. The same basic form enables very diverse organisations.[2]

2.1 Individual Rights and Joint Action

Kant recognises a range of individual rights. Reflecting the core idea of innate right, we have rights to bodily integrity, including freedoms to move and to speak (6:237 f). We can also 'acquire' three further forms of right.

We may own *property*: we acquire things and land, for example. We can make *contracts* with other people: we acquire rights that other people perform specific actions, such as repaying a debt. We can also gain rights concerning another person's *status*. Kant suggests this right applies only to domestic contexts – for example, when two people marry they acquire rights over one another. Later, I will suggest that employment can be understood in related terms (§4.4).

These rights give us the freedom to make many individual decisions. I can decide what to do in my flat, for example, or how to dispose of my time. These rights also allow us to associate with other people, if they agree. For example, people are free to form friendships, in line with their individual and shared ethical judgements.

Contract and status rights create enforceable obligations. A contract enables us to count on specific actions: you will deliver cakes next week, for example, and I will pay you. Status rights give legal form to lasting relationships. Friends have no legal rights over one another. But spouses can make arrangements for each other – for example, regarding the marital home.

---

[2] For simplicity, I treat artificial legal personality as an all-or-nothing matter. But there are some in-between possibilities. Law may grant certain aspects of independent legal personality to otherwise private arrangements: e.g. unincorporated associations, limited liability partnerships, and some trusts and charitable foundations. In the other direction, some state institutions enjoy (some) independence from the state: e.g. so-called 'quangos' in the UK or German public universities.

2.1.1 Two Limits of Law

Legal commitments help people sustain joint projects. But they can also give cause for regret – even in simple contracts, never mind marriage. As Onora O'Neill stresses, consent is 'opaque' (1984: 174 f, 1985: 255 f). We can't fully 'see through' the letter of our agreement to every implication; no one can see the future. Adding conditions to a contract may help, but it also makes scope for new complications.

At the start of the *Metaphysics of Morals* (6:233–6), Kant stresses two limits of law. These can, he says, make the concept of 'right' seem ambiguous. He illustrates the first with exactly this problem. If people go into business together, it makes sense to clarify commitments in writing – a partnership contract. This guards against some disappointments. Partners must live up to their commitments, or they can be forced to pay compensation.

But other disappointments are possible. In Kant's example, the agreed division of profits and losses may not reflect actual contributions – a problem of 'equity'. However complex, no contract could take account of every factor that bears on actual developments. But courts must uphold rights as written in the contract.

More broadly, long-term joint activities depend on two things that are hard to combine. We must be able to count on other people. We must be able to revise our goals and methods. Circumstances may change; we may change our minds.

This relates to a second limit of law, concerning the power of coercion. Kant's illustration concerns the crime of murder. In general, the threat of punishment outweighs anything we might gain by disobeying this prohibition. But this is not always true. Kant gives the example of a ship-wrecked sailor who can save his own life only by murdering someone else. For Kant, this limits law's power to punish, since even the death penalty cannot deter (6:235 f). I want to note a related problem in private law.

Joint activities rest on active contributions: business partners must *do business* together. If a partner no longer feels committed, or lacks the necessary abilities, the threat of force is of limited use. For one thing, the threat is more limited than in criminal law. Civil wrongs are enforced by compensation, not bodily coercion. Even if this were not the case, threats are not a good way to create enthusiasm or skill. In other words, law can only play a limited role in upholding joint action. It helps, but disappointments are still possible.

Many disappointments reflect the fact that private law relates named individuals: people with limitations and eccentricities and competing priorities. When we make a simple contract, we can ignore many of these factors: we only promise a few actions (delivering the cake, paying the bill). Marriage lies at the other extreme: these are *personal* arrangements, mutually fulfilling only so long as the parties are well-matched. Business partnerships are not so far from marriage: to work well, they depend on factors that are hard or impossible to enforce.

2.1.2 Private Right and the Limits of Shared Property

As noted, private rights bind named persons. Death brings things to an end; loss of commitment may do so, too. In addition, the parties have rights and duties beyond their relationship. This can also create problems. To illustrate, consider the role of property in many shared activities.

For example, when two people become business partners, both usually invest some money. In Kant's day, two merchants might buy a ship together. They authorise one another to use and manage this. As a useful object, this 'joint stock' is indivisible. Legally, the ship belongs to the partners, *not* the partnership. It cannot: a partnership is a relationship; it has no rights of its own.

Now consider the case where one partner incurs personal debts. Their creditor seeks repayment. A debt contract is legally enforceable. If this partner's only remaining asset is their share in the ship, then the courts will force its sale. This sinks the partnership, and probably the business prospects of the other partner. Law stands by people's rights; the partnership has none.

The partners can take some precautions. For example: ask lenders to agree to special loan contracts that exclude business assets. But there is a deeper difficulty: some duties are not negotiable. One partner may incur a legal duty to compensate someone for damage or injury, separately from his activities as a business partner. The injured party never agreed to be injured, hence never agreed to exempt the business assets of their injurer.

Related problems used to affect social insurance schemes. People might agree to make small payments each week, to create a fund to cover medical costs or care for dependents. But private agreements were inadequate. Legal frameworks were needed to separate this fund from individual property and create remedies for abuse (National Co-operative Archive 2014: 24 f).

These difficulties reflect the underlying structure of private right. This recognises people as unified bearers of rights and duties. If I own something – a share in a ship, for example – then it is also a means by which I can discharge my duties. Even if they are physically unified, shared assets must be legally divisible. When push comes to shove, this may require a fire sale that goes against the interests of all (co-)owners.

So private right can be frustrating for joint activities. People are mortal; no one is completely reliable; everyone has other obligations. Many useful things function as wholes: not just ships, but landed estates and churches, warehouses and factories, research facilities and university campuses. These enable many long-term cooperative activities, just as they require many people to develop and use them over long periods. There are strong practical reasons to separate them from individuals.

2.2 Corporations as Artificial Legal Persons: A Bare Kantian Outline

Among many controversies, here are two certainties about corporations. They are formed out of people. They are legal entities – that is, they have legal rights and duties, distinct from those of individual people.

In Kant's day, corporations were sometimes called 'moral persons'. Now it is more usual to call them 'legal' or 'artificial persons'. Either way, the contrast is with human beings or 'natural persons'.

Corporations are 'legal persons' because they have legal rights and duties. Like you and me, a corporation must act in line with these: in the old-fashioned legal phrase, it can 'sue and be sued'. Since flesh-and-blood people are sometimes also called 'legal persons' (Kurki 2023), I will refer to corporations as 'artificial persons': legal entities that exist 'only in contemplation of law' (*Trustees of Dartmouth College* 1819: 636).[3]

Kant does not spell the point out, but his foundational principle of innate equality has major implications for artificial persons. Corporations do not depend on any specific natural person; but people must act for them. When someone exercises a corporation's legal powers, this poses a fundamental threat to innate equality. This requires justifications and conditions, which must go beyond private right.

2.2.1 Participation and Corporate (Im)mortality

An artificial person has no natural existence or mortal body: innate right cannot apply. Kant's innate freedom and equality apply only to actual, flesh-and-blood persons. People should be free to set and pursue their own ends. They should be equal members of the state, so they must be accorded rights as citizens.

---

[3] Since people must act on behalf of the corporation, 'only' may be too strong. Lurking here is an old debate as to whether corporations are 'real' or 'fictional': does corporate law recognise pre-existing social groups, or does it deal merely with its own creations? (Paton 1972: §90, 'Theories of the Nature of Corporate Personality'). Arguably, much depends on the type of organisation and its specific history: the sociological 'matter' behind the legal 'form' varies enormously. Contrast, for examples, 'societies' that may exist in a state of nature (6:306) with nobilities, 'conceivable only within the state' (6:370; §3.3.2).

By definition, artificial legal persons have rights and duties before the law – above all, acquired rights to own, contract, and employ. But it would be a category mistake to place artificial persons on the same footing as living persons and citizens. A corporation cannot vote in elections, for example. Nor is it free to set its own purposes (§2.4.2).

Still, a corporation always depends on actual people. An artificial person can only act if natural persons *act for it*. A range of relationships make this possible: offices, membership, and employment are the most important.

In every corporation, some people must have authority to make corporate decisions. A board of trustees or an executive officer may act for the corporation. They act as corporate *agents*, in the legal sense of that word: they act *on behalf of* the corporation; it is their *principal*. This also means that they have duties to act in terms of corporate purposes and policies.

In most cases, a corporation also has *members*, who *belong to it*. Obviously, this is not a property relation: people may never be *owned*. Instead, it points to a relationship with rights and obligations on both sides. If the members belong to the trade union, we can also say that the union *belongs to them*. But again: the corporation is not their property. They also have duties towards it and within it, just as officers or trustees do. (In Section 4, on business corporations, I will say more about the idea of corporations as property, since it is common to speak of people 'owning' businesses: §4.1.4.)

A third relationship is employment (again, more on this later: §4.4). Workers *act for* most types of corporation, usually with more limited powers than trustees or officers.

In different ways, offices, membership, and employment 'incorporate' people: people gain powers to act for and within the corporation. Instead of a living body, a corporation has living people who act for it.

Since those people may be replaced, corporations are potentially immortal. Here is Blackstone's moving description:

> for all the individual members that have existed from the foundation [of the corporation] to the present time, or that shall ever hereafter exist, are but one person in law, a person that never dies: in like manner as the river Thames is still the same river, though the parts which compose it are changing every instant. (1765: 468)

Members and officers may leave the trade union, for example, but the union persists so long as other people keep it going.

Contrast the forms of joint action possible under private right. In general, they end when someone dies. Marriage is absolutely personal: no substitutes! Contracts may be more impersonal, but they are between named persons.

A substitution means renegotiation. It is quite different with corporations: people come and go; the artificial person 'never dies'.

But never say 'never'. Innate right cannot apply to an artificial person, but a corporation certainly has acquired rights. So it must fulfil the corresponding duties. For example, a corporation must pay what it owes, or creditors may take it to court. If the corporation cannot pay and no one will bail it out, then it is bankrupt. A natural person can pick up the pieces after they go bankrupt. An artificial person loses its capacities completely. Its rights are *only* acquired: they can all be lost. This is one sort of corporate death. It is especially important in competitive contexts, as I stress in Section 4 on business corporations.

2.2.2 Artificial Personhood, Innate Equality, and Personal Liability

In the Introduction, I underlined the fundamental place of Kantian innate right (§1.3.2). A legal system is only rightful if it upholds everyone's freedom – that is, their 'independence from being bound by others to more than one can in turn bind them' (6:237).

Legal equality means we are all 'bound' equally. We must all respect each other's persons and property – that is, we cannot use private coercion to bind others. We may all enter into contracts; when we do, we are each bound to fulfil our part of the contract. In each case, the legal system ensures that no one is bound more than others 'can in turn bind them'. Only lawful force binds us, all to the same degree. Artificial persons attack this equality at its roots.

Actual, flesh-and-blood people must act if a corporation is to use its property or engage in contractual relations. But if the corporation is the legal actor, then the corporation is legally responsible. Except for serious carelessness or fraud, the people involved are not (§2.4.5).

Here is an historical illustration. The Dutch East India Company was created by a public licence or *Octrooi* in 1602. To start with, the Company seemed to be some sort of complicated, state-sponsored cartel (Ciepley 2023: 860). For example, the leading merchants signed its debt contracts. If funds ran short, they were personally liable.

As borrowing needs mounted, the merchants took a bold step (Gelderblom et al. 2013: 1070 ff). They still arranged loans, but these were now signed by company officials. Together with political support for the Company, this made the legal situation clear. The merchants were not private individuals. They were directors acting for a corporation. The Company was liable for the loans; they were not.

This was a new way of doing business, but the principle was well-established. Every corporation is a legal person *in its own right*, with its own assets and liabilities. Long before the Dutch Company, many other types of corporation existed: townships, universities, guilds, and monasteries. The same principle applies to every type of corporation invented since. The corporation acts *on its own account* – literally, in the case of loans.

In terms of Kant's innate equality, I want to stress how scandalous this is. Artificial legal persons enable some people to gain additional legal powers *without* bearing legal liability. When people act for corporations, they exercise powers 'to bind' which are distinct from their own private rights; yet they are not 'bound to' the corresponding duties and liabilities.

If *innate equality* means anything, no one should be able to multiply their legal agency. If being *equally bound* means anything, no one should be able to avoid legal liability.

Kant's contemporaries took note. The French Revolution proclaimed the principle of equal liberty, and drew the logical conclusion: no one should have extra rights to act through or for a corporation. The guillotine came down on corporations of all sorts – nobilities and feudal bodies, religious estates, guilds and trade organisations, and worker associations (Doyle 2019: Ch. 4).

Kant makes only one explicit remark. The new regime did no wrong in abolishing church estates: 'the state can cast off this burden ... when it wants to' (6:369). The same logic informs his insistence on the public's rights to reform and dismantle other corporations (Maliks 2022: 4, 32; §3.1.2). But he does not make the revolutionary call for wholesale abolition (§2.3).

One benefit of a Kantian approach, I believe, is that we must address the revolutionary challenge head-on. Why should people who demand equal freedom as their birthright also accept that some people command the powers, privileges, and protections accorded by artificial legal persons?

2.2.3 Corporations Threaten Innate Equality; Terms and Conditions Must Apply

The rest of this Element develops Kant's answer to this question, and extends it to some types of corporation that he did not know. As a first step, let me note some familiar limits and justifications which apply to the point I have just emphasised: that people are not liable ('bound') when they act for a corporation. While Kant barely hints at these points, they help explain why we rarely feel scandalised by corporate powers.

First, law recognises that people may act together. I can be an accomplice to your crime, for example. This principle also applies to corporations and the people who act for them. If a corporate officer or employee acts negligently, then both the individual and the corporation may be guilty.

Second, when I act for a corporation, I usually act with others. I take part in activities that go beyond what anyone could do individually, and often go beyond my knowledge (§3.2.4, §4.4.4). If people suffer damage or injury, it is often reasonable to make the organisation responsible. The corporation has wrongly 'bound' them; in return, compensation or other legal remedies bind the corporation to right the wrong.

Third, the corporation can exercise authority over the people who act for it. It does not have a court's coercive powers to imprison or to fine. But it has other important powers. Since it exercises property rights (for example, over its funds and buildings), it can reward someone or refuse hoped-for benefits. A corporation also has powers that have no parallel in private right: it can redefine and reallocate roles, for example, or expel or demote someone. I will say more about this corporate government in §§2.4.4–5.

These points suggest grounds for shifting and sharing responsibility. When we act for corporations, we act with others; we may face some personal liability in court; we may be accountable within the corporation.

Here is another, crucial justification for shifting responsibility from individuals to artificial persons, implicit in Kant's essay, 'What is Enlightenment?' (§2.3). People should be able to run a charity or church or university without risk to their own property and person. Honesty and competence cannot guarantee that complex activities will go to plan. If we undertake such duties, there should be a line between these and our private lives. Kantian private right sees the person as a unity. When we act for a worthwhile organisation, there must be some separation.

From a Kantian perspective, the point is that people may not decide this privately. It may be reasonable to share responsibility with a distinct artificial person, or to shift it entirely. There may be good reasons for some people to have additional legal powers to pursue various collaborative activities; there may be good reasons to let corporations hold them responsible, rather than the courts.

But it is not for me or for any group of private persons, to decide how far we are legally responsible for what we do. Deciding for oneself is the opposite of 'being bound by others' (6:237).

2.2.4 Recap: Private Law's Limitations and the Power of Artificial Legal Personality

A famous phrase of Kant's expresses the basic structure of private law. Describing reason as essentially *free*, he says that each person must be able 'to express his reservations, indeed even his veto ...' (*Critique of Pure Reason* A738 f/B766 f). People who come together freely can also part ways: friends drift apart; people decide not to renew a contract. This veto protects all individuals, equally. But it is costly for joint action.

The corporate form addresses this problem. An enduring artificial person enables long-term collaboration. By exercising acquired rights to property and contract, the corporation can build up and manage dedicated resources. People act for the corporation; they can come and go; the corporation survives. Every type of corporation brings a massive increase in social power.

But corporations also reshape our framework of legal responsibility. People no longer act as private individuals, equally free and equally bound. As officers and directors and trustees, as members or employees or volunteers, they take on new powers, new responsibilities, and changed liabilities.

These familiar aspects of organisational life are in deep tension with Kantian innate equality. They rest on powers beyond Kantian private right; they demand public justification and careful safeguards.

2.3 Corporations in Kant's Works

Kant considers several types of corporations. He also observes an important problem with the creation and control of artificial persons.

Conflict of the Faculties discusses universities. *Religion within the Boundaries of Mere Reason* discusses churches. Section 3 considers his arguments in more detail. In the *Metaphysics of Morals*, Kant examines various social and political associations. He briefly discusses nobilities (again, more on these in Section 3) and adds an important section on charitable foundations (more on these in a moment).

'What Is Enlightenment?' raises another aspect. The essay distinguishes two kinds of reasoning. Free citizens reason 'publicly', in the wider cause of enlightenment and civic progress. When someone acts for an organisation or the state, they make 'private use of reason' (8:37). Participants must act in terms of corporate purposes, policies, and roles, deciding how to fulfil organisational goals and instructions (§4.2.1, §4.4.4).

Kant also makes some passing comments. The most important concerns the 'trading companies' of the 'civilised, especially commercial, states' (*PP* 8:358 f). These included the Dutch and English East India Companies – ancestors of modern business corporations (§4.1.1).

Kant was aware of other types of corporation. Guilds for different trades still existed as corporate bodies. Freemasonry was organised through corporations – Kant was not a member, but many acquaintances were (Kuehn 2001: 225 f).

Many townships were 'municipal corporations' – a term still used in Britain fifty years ago.

Some of these corporations were becoming feudal relics even as Kant wrote – we feel no shock at the Revolution's attack on guilds and nobilities (§2.2.2). Other types of corporation have grown in importance – universities and charities, for instance.

New types of corporation have emerged since Kant's death. These include the defining institutions of modern societies: business corporations (Section 4) and political parties (§3.1.2). There are also: co-operatives; 'friendly societies' for mutual aid and social insurance; trade unions; pressure groups and other 'non-governmental organisations'.

Even in Kant's time, however, the diversity and flexibility of corporations was remarkable – as were some problems.

2.3.1 Charitable Foundations in the Metaphysics of Morals

On Kant's account of public right, the state is 'supreme proprietor' or *Obereigenthümer* of a given territory (6:323). This does not mean it *owns* the territory: the state is above ('*ober*') private property ('*Eigentum*').

As part of its 'supremacy', Kant holds that the state can 'repeal [corporations] at any time', just so long as 'it compensates those still alive' (6:324) – that is, so long as it respects people's private rights. As examples, he mentions knightly orders and church estates (6:324 f). Although corporations are potentially immortal, they have no right to live forever: only the state is 'perpetual' (6:326).

Kant added an Appendix to the second edition, published the following year. For the most part, this is a response to an early review of the book (Bouterwek 2014 [1797]). But it includes several pages (6:367–70) on 'perpetual foundations', although the review said nothing about these.

Kant doubles down on his position. No corporation has rights to exist in perpetuity. Reform and abolition do not go against private right or wrong the original founder's 'appointed heir' (6:367). As well as religious estates, he considers foundations for needy persons, nobilities, and entailed estates. Section 3 takes up Kant's claims. Here I note the kerfuffle that led Kant to revisit the topic, which brings out much wider issues about corporate purposes and governance (§2.4).

The story was told by Otto Gradenwitz (1904). When Professor Kypke of the University of Königsberg died, he left a bequest for a charitable foundation providing student housing. In 1796–7, the University Senate oversaw the necessary arrangements. Kant was still a senator: old, frail, preoccupied with the *Metaphysics of Morals*, but proud of his position.

Kypke's will created a corporate zombie. As a private individual or single member of the Senate, Kypke never had the right to govern student housing. Yet his dying will gives birth to a new legal person, governing people and resources after his death, without capacities for judgement or revision. The supervisor and residents should act on Kypke's terms: strict requirements on the residents (to be checked upon every evening, or they would lose their place in the home); a generous salary and accommodation for the supervisor (which led to awkward discussions in the Senate, since the University Chancellor applied for this cushy position). Ethically, the arrangements were unfair and restrictive. Even if they were not, they might become unhelpful or irrelevant as circumstances change (Gradenwitz 1904: 194 ff).

The foundation is an unholy mixture of private rights (to donate property, to act in line with your own ethical judgement), corporate powers (to govern university members), and powers that no one should ever have (to govern people and resources in perpetuity, divorced from on-going practical judgement and possible progress). Law keeps the zombie lurching on, although the wrong-headed spirit is dead.

2.3.2 How Can We Pass on Shared Goods?

This minor difficulty at Kant's university highlights a profound issue: how can people bequeath shared goods to future generations?

Kant starts with the claim that a 'rightful condition' must be perpetual, because individual rights should never be insecure. But individual rights are for mortal human beings. We may hope for a future life, but our time on earth is limited. Among other rights, individuals can make bequests; beneficiaries make their own decisions in turn. Civic rights enable people to contribute to social progress. For example, by the 'public use of reason', Kant hopes that citizens can improve political arrangements: 'perpetual' does not mean unchangeable.

A 'perpetual foundation' disrupts the division between mortal human beings and perpetual state. Legal arrangements uphold the wishes of the dead, rather than the rights of the living. Applied to land, medieval law called this 'mortmain': the 'dead hand' of the past. Kypke uses rights he acquired in life (significant wealth) to create an 'immortality' (6:369) that mere mortals must lack. The 'artificial person' betrays innate freedom and equality: a dead person's will binds the hands of living people.

At the same time, there must be ways to pass on shared goods – as the University of Königsberg did, for example. A long-term endeavour spanned generations, though people came and went. In other words, the problems with

Kypke's foundation are not arguments against artificial persons, simply as such. Kant only insists on the state's right to repeal or reform corporations.

Section 3 develops Kant's arguments for some types of corporation and against others. In the rest of this section, I highlight three features that every corporation must have, if it is to avoid Kypke's problems. Alongside legal personality and its acquired rights, corporations require: *purpose*; *participation*; and *governmental powers*.

2.4 Corporations, Private Contracts, and 'Social Contracts'

Two points follow directly from Kant's principle of innate equality and his understanding of our rights as private individuals. First, people cannot create corporations by exercising private rights such as property or contract. For example, Kypke's foundation depended on authorisation by the Prussian state: he exercised a (badly framed) *civic* right (§1.3.3, §2.5.2), not just his private right to bequeath property. Second, people should not be able to direct a corporation in line with their private ends: this would give them unequal powers to bind others. This means a corporation must have a purpose of its own.

I will explain both points in terms of the difference between a corporation and a private contract. Contracts enable many cooperative activities – for example, purchases, loans, and partnership. However, they cannot give rise to a distinct, artificial legal person.

Before going into detail, let me note one form of private right that may have a corporate aspect. *Domestic right* comprises marriage, parenthood, and master-servant relations. For Kant, these constitute the household. They create something akin to a corporate entity: a 'society of members of a whole' (6:276), or as Helga Varden puts it, 'a legally recognized personal "us"' with a shared home (2020: 253 ff).

This 'whole' or 'us' depends on a feature that is present in domestic right, but not contract (see also §§4.4.1–2). This is the power to bind people in terms of legally recognised purposes. Parents govern children to ensure their care and development. The master governs servants for the 'welfare of the household' (6:360).

Kant's own interpretation of domestic right creates a sexist autocracy: the male head of household *rules* wife and servants. No modern commentator thinks this is compatible with innate equality. (As well as Varden 2020, see Moran 2021, Pascoe 2022: 8 ff, Vrousalis 2022.) But this problem sets an important challenge. Can governmental relations support equality, rather than attack it?

2.4.1 States as Corporations Based on a Social Contract

Corporations bring people together as a single body. The same idea applies to states: they unite citizens as a 'body politic'. Kant's main example of a 'moral person' is the state (6:341, 343); just once, he refers to states as '*Corporationen*' (6:350).

Kant draws on a famous metaphor in political theory: the state as *social contract*. But there is a radical difference between private contracts and 'social' ones. Only the social contract creates a corporation (Ciepley 2017).

Private contracts bring two or more people together in an exchange. Each offers something; each accepts something. In doing so, as Kant says, the parties 'unite' their wills (6:274). They act *as one* in agreeing. Each is 'bound' equally: to deliver their side of the bargain.

At first sight, Kant's account of the social contract is remarkably similar. There is an exchange. When people become citizens, they give up the 'lawless freedom' of the state of nature, in exchange for 'freedom ... in a juridical condition' (6:316). There is also a 'united will'. The 'general united will of the people' creates the state (6:313 ff).

Every social contract theorist is aware of one difference. No one actually makes this 'contract'. Many controversies focus on the gulf between real and imagined agreement. Kant's response is to argue that we *must* agree to political authority, and that political authority is legitimate so long as our consent is *possible*. (I return to this idea in §3.3.)

There is another difference, less often noticed. Who takes part in the contract? – In private contracts, this is clear. Actual people agree; actual people do what they agreed. (Or can be taken to court, if they fail.) The social contract is different. It grants us 'freedom in a juridical condition'. But it needs a new type of 'person' to deliver on the bargain. Strange to tell, the people who make the contract cannot deliver what they promise one another.

Before the imagined contract, there are people in the plural, considered as individuals (*vereinzelt*: 6:315). With 'the idea of this [contract]' (6:315), there is *the* people, singular: constituted as a state or moral person. To recall Kant's book title, this new entity is a 'foundational' element of the metaphysics of right. Only the state can deliver 'freedom in a juridical condition'.

This may be why Kant refers to an 'original contract' (6:315, 340). Unlike private contract, the social contract is the 'origin' of a new actor, the state.

For the same reason, 'united will' now has a different meaning. In a private contract, this 'will' is the parties' agreement that each will do their part. Their wills unite on this point. Still, they remain separate *parties*, each with their own reasons for taking part. They do not share a purpose. There is no new actor with its own will.

By contrast, the social contract creates a state with its own powers of action. Citizens are not separate parties. Instead, they *belong to* the state as '*members, united for legislating*' – that is, for an overarching purpose (6:314, my emphasis). Only this new 'moral person' can deliver a condition of equal freedom.

In sum, private contracts differ from the social contract at a fundamental, metaphysical level. Only the social contract constitutes a new moral person. This entity has a governing purpose ('freedom in a juridical condition'); membership (citizens); and a constitution (ideally, for Kant, a republican one: §3.1.2). Only then is Kant's 'power to bind', or govern, compatible with each person's innate right to freedom.

In what follows, I show why ordinary corporations – that is, artificial legal persons below the state – must have some similar features. Anything else would betray innate equality.

2.4.2 Artificial Persons Must Have a Defined Purpose

As we have seen (§2.2.2), artificial persons challenge innate equality. When people act for an artificial person, they do not face the same liabilities as private individuals. They gain additional legal powers: they may use the corporation's resources, help decide its actions and policies, or govern other participants.

At the level of the state, Kant's response is simple, at least in principle. We should distinguish *personal ends* from *public purposes*. Sovereigns may never treat ruling as a private prerogative (see 'Perpetual Peace', especially). State officials must use their powers for public purposes.

Of course, the people involved still have ordinary motives and incentives. Civil servants may do their jobs because they want the salary. Their roles may involve the sort of tasks needed to keep any organisation going: their connection to public responsibilities is indirect. Alternatively, an official may care deeply about their public responsibilities. We might hesitate to speak of their commitment as 'private', because they have taken public purposes to heart. But it still makes sense to speak of their *personal* ends, as distinct from public purposes achieved through institutional cooperation.

In each case, we should be able to see the official's conduct as contributing to a public purpose (Ripstein 2009: 193). The alternative is corruption: the private abuse of public office.

I suggest a parallel idea must apply to corporations. As Kant assumes of each corporate form he endorses (§3.1, §3.2), a corporation must have a defined purpose. Otherwise, the artificial legal actor would be *merely a means* for people to pursue their personal ends. Some people would be able to exercise additional legal powers, without the same liability they would face as private individuals. This cannot be: it would betray innate equality.

Or to put the same point in reverse. When someone acts for or within a corporation, we should be able to understand their conduct in terms of corporate purpose. If not, they use the corporation's legal powers and protections *merely* as means to their personal or private ends.

As before, the people involved have ordinary motives and incentives. They might enjoy the status or recognition or power, for example. Alternatively, they may care deeply about the corporation's purpose. Like the committed public servant, a trustee may be dedicated to their charity's cause, for example; they may even have founded the charity to pursue this commitment. Their personal ends align with the corporate purpose. Founding and governing the charity is a *means* for them to further a cause they care about.

However, the charity must not be *merely a means*. The trustee's commitments may change. This is part of innate freedom: everyone may decide on new priorities and different ends. Still, the trustee cannot use the charity's powers as a means to their new cause. They can only exercise *their own* rights to support this – with their personal resources, or even by exercising the civic right to found a new charity.

The formal point is this: Kantian right cannot authorise legal persons merely as means for people to extend their private agency – be this selfish or public-spirited. So corporations must have a defined purpose. The purpose cannot be so narrow that it defeats intelligent response to changing circumstances. (Recall Kypke's zombie.) It must not be so broad that it allows people to make the corporation a mere means for their personal ends. Sections 3 and 4 will consider a range of purposes, and how these justify different types of corporation.

2.4.3 Artificial Persons Must Have People Who Act for Them

A second formal constraint follows from the fact that an artificial person has no living body: natural persons must act for it. There must be ways to recruit participants: officers, members, employees. There must be ways for people to leave.

Again, this has no parallel with private contract. A contract is *between* the parties; it is not a distinct entity. To add or replace someone requires a new contract. This requires the consent of all the parties: in effect, each has a veto. Likewise, one or more contracting parties cannot decide to expel another: each is equally bound by their commitment; there is nothing to expel them *from*.

The analogy between states and other corporations is only partial. Kant insists that everyone must belong to a state. This 'must' has two sides. No one should be left without citizenship: this follows from innate right. Each person must submit to the state's authority. Unlike any private contract, the 'social contract' is obligatory.

For the most part, corporate participation is voluntary; there is no innate right to belong. So the agreement is two-sided. People can join if they wish *and* if the corporation is willing to admit them. The same point also implies that people can leave, in line with their personal wishes and priorities. Or people can be expelled, if the corporation is no longer willing to have them.

But how is a corporation to decide who to admit or to expel? This cannot be a personal decision: a corporation cannot be an extension of someone's private will. So it requires procedures that reflect the purpose of the corporation and the means it has to pursue those purposes.

We know these procedures vary enormously, just as modes of participation vary – in terms of duties, rights, benefits, and powers. Again, I just want to emphasise the formal point. Incorporating people into an artificial person is a legal matter, involving new powers and changed liabilities.[4]

2.4.4 Artificial Persons Require Government

This points to a third feature. There must be a constitution to enable corporate decisions and to structure activity over the long-term.

Again, contrast a private contract. The parties decide their duties at the start. Each party is bound to fulfil these – no less and no more. The contract can be complex: some duties may only apply in specified circumstances; in longer-term contracts, there may be duties to coordinate.

Still, we should not speak of government. If the parties disagree as to what the contract requires, there is an impasse; in the limit, they can go to court if they think another party has failed to do their part. But one party cannot *redefine* the other party's duties. One party cannot *decide* that the other has failed. As regards their participants, corporations do both.

First, the corporation must pursue its purpose: it must act intelligently and flexibly, in the face of changing circumstances. So it must be able to specify and revise participants' rights and duties. There must be ways to decide who can act and speak for the corporation – to make contracts, for example, or represent it in court. Both aspects require some sort of constitution: a charter or articles of association.

---

[4] Ripstein (2009: 73 ff) and Castro (2014) suggest that Kant's status right points to the form of such relations. In §4.4, I take up this idea in relation to employment.

Second, a corporation must be able to judge whether participants are living up to their responsibilities – to pursue its purpose, meet its legal obligations, and act in terms of its constitution. A new sphere of corporate accountability opens up. There must be ways to deal with people who disregard or damage the corporation's pursuit of its purpose. There must be ways to ensure that people do not turn the corporation into a mere means for their private purposes.

2.4.5 But Can Corporations Really 'Govern' Participants?

Since modern corporations cannot coerce people or prevent them from leaving,[5] we might wonder how far corporations can really *govern*. Here are two ways to see the extent of their powers. (See also Anderson 2017, Ciepley 2023.)

First, people may benefit from participation, or even rely on it. Some benefits may be extrinsic – wages, for example. Other benefits relate to participation but not specific corporate purposes. I may find it rewarding to develop or exercise specific skills; membership may involve a valuable social status.

Often, the connection goes deeper. I have pointed out that personal ends may align with corporate purposes, or even be shaped by these. Kant's own position as Professor and Senator can illustrate. He observes that a scholar may live 'in a state of nature so far as learning is concerned ... working by himself, as an *amateur* and without public precepts or rules' (7:18). However, the 'amateur' cannot take part in academic life, in ways that Kant himself was personally committed to.

Second, resignation or expulsion has definitive legal consequences. The ex-participant no longer enjoys corporate benefits and powers. In the unlikely case they can get around this forcible exclusion, they are liable to charges of trespass and theft.

The same applies to demotion. For example, the constitution may empower some participants to vote on official appointments. If they disapprove of the officers' conduct (the borrowing decisions mentioned in §2.2.2, say), they may elect different officers. The debt still belongs to the corporation: the members cannot make the previous officers liable for it. But removal from office holds them accountable in a different way (§2.2.3).

In all these cases, the corporation exercises legal rights over people and property. As Kant insists, rights are connected with an authorisation to coerce (6:231). This power may not be directly corporal, but it still binds (§1.3.3). It alters opportunities and privileges; sometimes it takes them away entirely.

---

[5] Early and pre-modern corporations sometimes claimed these rights. For example, the English East India Company's charters laid down extensive powers of corporal punishment and implied powers of colonial conquest (§4.1.1). I also mention Kant's example of feudal corporations in §3.3.2 and an inquisitor in §3.4.3. All fundamentally contradict Kantian principles.

In §4.4.2, I note a third aspect of corporate governance. Larger corporations structure activity – physically and epistemically, procedurally and organisationally.

2.4.6 Recap: Three Features of the 'Corporate Contract'

Corporations unite people as an artificial legal person. We may speak of a 'social contract' or even a 'corporate contract' (Easterbrook & Fischel 1989). But we should also note the fundamental difference from private contract: there is now a new legal actor. From the point of view of innate equality, this is a profound problem *and* a great relief.

It is a problem, because Kant starts with the principle that it is never rightful, for any individual to have unequal powers to bind others. Artificial persons can only act if living people act for them. So there is always a risk that living people will use corporate powers for merely private ends, undermining equal freedom.

It is a relief, because an artificial person can have a specific purpose and can govern participants through its legal and organisational structure. To the extent that people act for this purpose, we should not say that their private agency is extended. Instead, they contribute to the corporate purpose. So long as this purpose can be publicly justified, there is no insult to innate equality.

Let me emphasise that this point is not about the value of people's ends; it is about equal freedom. Consider Kant's own example of sovereigns who pursue their subjects' happiness. They are 'despots' (6:318, 339), just like rulers who oppress. This is not because Kant disapproves of happiness: as private individuals, we should promote other people's happiness (6:385 f). It is because governing *binds* people, and no one should be able to do this more than anyone else. So governing must always serve a public purpose. In the case of the state, which compels everyone, this must be each person's equal freedom.

In the case of non-state corporations, the problem is milder. They do not govern everyone in a given territory by coercive laws. Rather, corporations exercise acquired rights (property and contract) as well as powers to incorporate people (as officers, members, or employees).

Nonetheless, as soon as people can act for a corporation, they exercise additional powers to bind – that is, to act in ways that go beyond their rights as private individuals. This bears on everyone's rightful situation. Kant's approach is principled and formal. It cannot disregard this challenge to innate equality on the basis that many material effects will be desirable or that few corporations can match states' powers to act.

In sum, Kant does not draw the French revolutionaries' radical conclusion: liberty and equality demand wholesale corporate abolition. It is possible that his position is inconsistent – like his sexist, exclusionary, autocratic view of domestic right. I have suggested a different view: the structure of Kantian public right also shows how corporate structures can be legitimate. Section 3 will develop this point in a positive direction, arguing that some corporate structures are required by right.

2.5 How to Make Artificial Persons

We have just seen that private contracts cannot create an artificial legal person. This has a straightforward implication: only public right can give rise to artificial persons. However, this need not exclude private initiative.

History shows two ways of making corporations. One is a sovereign charter. The other is a legal framework that allows people to create a corporation by following standard procedures.

2.5.1 Sovereign Charter: The Old-Fashioned Way to Make a Corporation

In Kant's day, major corporations were based on an individual charter from the state. Often, merchants or townships petitioned the sovereign for the privilege of incorporation. A coat of arms marked this royal blessing.

Here is Elizabeth I, issuing the charter of the English East India Company in 1600:

> Know Ye Therefore, that we ... have of our especial Grace, certain Knowledge, and mere Motion, given and granted ... [that there] shall be one Body Corporate and Politick, in Deed and in Name, by the Name of The Governor and Company of Merchants of London, Trading into the East-Indies ... [They] may have a Common Seal, to serve for all the Causes and Business of them and their Successors .... (Shaw 1887: 2 f)

There are modern examples, too. Here is Elizabeth II, chartering Lancaster University in 1964:

> Now therefore know ye that We by virtue of Our Prerogative Royal and of Our especial grace, certain knowledge and mere motion have willed and ordained ... [that there] shall be one Body Politic and Corporate with perpetual succession and a Common Seal by the name and style of 'The University of Lancaster' ... (1964/2018: Schedule §§1–2)

The underlying ideas extend to every jurisdiction, despite the antiquated regal wording. Natural persons are born: they live by virtue of natural processes; no 'prerogative royal' is needed. Artificial persons exist by sovereign 'grace' – in other words, by virtue of public right. They live through the law's 'knowledge and motion'. Law *knows* the corporation by a singular 'name and style'. Law *moves* with corporate deeds. These are marked by a 'common seal', as opposed to a person's signature.

Such charters lay down a corporation's purpose. For example, 'The objects of [Lancaster] University shall be to advance knowledge, wisdom and understanding by teaching and research . . .' (Schedule §3).

Charters also lay down membership and governance procedures. For the University, there are specific offices and decision-making bodies (Court, Council, Senate). There is the power to appoint officers and govern members, and provisions to amend some aspects, subject to statutory approval.

Kant was familiar with all this. The 1544 charter of his university had the same form. Albrecht, Duke of Prussia created the *Königsberger Academie* by the authority vested in his office. A new legal body should exist, serve educational and religious purposes, and have the right to admit and govern members (Arnoldt 1746: *Beylagen Num.* 6).

2.5.2 Another Way to Make a Corporation: Authorisation by Standing Laws

For all its faults, Kypke's zombie shows a second route. Legal provisions may give individuals a civic right (§1.3.3) to create some types of corporation. As Kant notes, a foundation is 'voluntarily established': it arises at a private person's initiative. But the state must also 'confirm' it (6:367). Without this authorisation, Kypke's bequest would have no legal force.

Authorisation can take different forms. The 1794 Prussian legal code, for example, gives broad support: 'almshouses, hospitals, orphanages and foundling homes, work- and labour-houses stand under the special protection of the state'. The code confirms existing foundations and requires new foundations to be registered with the state. By default, the state will authorise them in line with the founder's wishes – unless this would be 'impossible or even harmful' (quoted Strachwitz 2010: 103).

Kant's discussion of perpetual corporations suggests that public right should be more cautious. Kypke's zombie illustrates the need for mechanisms to govern and reform, review and even abolish these bodies. Artificial personhood makes no sense without capacities for intelligent activity: purposive and responsive. A legal privilege cannot be an irrevocable gift (§2.3.2).

Modern legal frameworks take account of these issues. For example, charities law grants private individuals the civic right to create a charity. There is a range of constraints and safeguards. The founders must lay down a specific purpose that falls within the broad scope of 'public benefit'. That purpose is part of a constitution which also defines offices, membership, and governance. There is a statutory oversight body – in the UK, the Charity Commission. It reviews annual reports from all charities; it can investigate suspicions of misconduct; it can approve or reject changes to a charity's purposes. (See also §3.4.4.)

Parallel arrangements apply to most types of corporation in most jurisdictions. For political parties and trade unions, churches and cooperatives, legal frameworks allow people to create new artificial persons. Those laws set conditions, including constraints on purposes, participation and governance, as well as ways to revise these. Participants take most decisions without direct state involvement. Legal frameworks provide modes of oversight and accountability, as well as channels to address complaints.

Although we rarely appreciate it, business corporations also rely on standing laws. Section 4 insists on this point and its importance. Corporate markets can only exist through public right. The ways in which business is incorporated therefore require public justification.

Conclusion to Section 2

Kant's *Groundwork* argues that people are ends-in-themselves; they must never be *mere means* (§1.3). The *Doctrine of Right* protects people against such *misuse*: innate and acquired rights enable people to govern their own lives. The *Doctrine of Virtue* adds: each person has the duty to be a 'useful member of the world' (6:446) – or in other words, to act as a means (not *mere means*!) to worthwhile ends.

This does not address how people can come together to pursue lasting collective projects. Kantian private right safeguards freedom and protects us against instrumentalisation. We can decide to associate and cooperate with others; we can also walk away. Contracts only introduce limited commitments. These safeguards make us less useful for joint activities.

Corporate organisation overcomes these difficulties. Artificial legal persons govern people to pursue specified purposes over the long term. They use corporate resources rather than jointly owned property. Individuals need only participate so long as they are willing. When people do this – and especially when they act as officers or directors – they take on additional legal powers, with reduced legal liability. We rarely notice this, let alone find it scandalous.

This is not, I suggest, because we doubt Kant's fundamental principle – that no one should be 'bound by others to more than one can in turn bind them' (6:237). Civic equality was revolutionary in Kant's day, but no longer. More likely, I think, is that we take corporate powers for granted, as well as some familiar safeguards and justifications. The next section considers Kant's justifications for corporations based on a range of purposes, as well as some further cautions.

3 Justifications and Safeguards

Section 2 argued that corporations stand in profound tension with innate equality. They require that some people take on additional legal powers, while modifying those people's liabilities. To preserve equal freedom, those powers must be exercised, not for private ends, but for publicly justifiable purposes. This section turns to Kant's justifications for some corporate purposes, and the safeguards that must accompany these.

The first two parts consider arguments for incorporation based on purposes that Kant explicitly endorses. For the sake of right (§3.1), some powers must be separate from the state: universities, for example. I tie this example to wider arguments about democracy and public right. For the sake of virtue (§3.2), other powers must be separate too – for example, religious congregation and charity. As legal entities, such corporations connect right and virtue.

Alongside specific purposes, Kant suggests two lines of thought that may provide broader support for incorporation. However, both approaches also call for strict cautions.

Kant argues that states may legislate as they see fit, just so long as citizens *could* consent to such laws (§3.3). However, Kant also insists that feudal corporate arrangements fail this test. That is, some corporate purposes go directly against his principles. I point out that such arrangements corrupt virtue as well as right.

Not least, freedom is fundamental to Kant's theory. Civic rights to form corporations promise to extend freedom (§3.4). However, such rights must be compatible with *equal* freedom. As well as setting limits on corporate purposes, this implies that states have special duties to 'police' corporate activity, as Kant puts it. Corporations act at *arm's length* from the state; but this cannot mean *beyond reach*. There must be channels for oversight, reform, and democratic accountability.

3.1 Public Right Requires Some Types of Corporation

Kant was a proud and active member of one corporation: the University of Königsberg (§2.3.1). His writings on universities and public reasoning suggest the following argument. Many tasks are essential to a rightful condition. States must undertake some of these directly – criminal justice, for example. (And much else: Cordelli 2020.) However, other tasks must be separate from the state – the pursuit of knowledge, for example. Incorporation allows long-term collective action towards these ends.

3.1.1 Public Right and the Purpose of Knowledge

Kant discusses universities in *The Conflict of the Faculties*. They are 'public institutions'; they must also have 'a certain autonomy' (7:17). This autonomy is especially marked in the 'philosophy faculty', by which Kant means the whole domain of scholarly and scientific enquiry (7:28 f). The free examination of knowledge claims is essential both to science and the public use of reason (7:20).

Kant's phrase, 'a certain autonomy', was not casual: academic freedom was close to his heart. In the 1770s and 1780s, he corresponded with the reforming minister of education, Karl Abraham von Zedlitz (dedicatee of the first *Critique*; Hochstrasser 2000: 189–197). After the death of Frederick the Great in 1786, Kant was concerned about state influence within his university (Euler & Stiening 1995: 67). In the 1790s, the Prussian state censor condemned his writings on religion. Kant knew the stakes in both academic and ecclesiastical (§3.2.2) separations of power.

As well as founding universities (§2.5.1), the state takes a special interest in the faculties of theology, medicine, and law. These serve specific public needs (for instance, licensing doctors and lawyers). To some extent, then, they must answer to the government (7:26, 34 f). At the same time, they must answer to truth and reason. So they must be combined with free scientific enquiry – that is, placed within universities. Kant likens the philosophy faculty to an 'opposition party': it does not play a governmental role; but it has the duty to speak freely (see also *PP* 8:368 ff). More colloquially, its task is to keep others *honest*.

Kant's famous discussion of the 'public use of reason' (in 'What Is Enlightenment?') hints at the tasks needed for democracy. Citizens must be able to criticise policies and institutions, and to discuss possible reforms. Those discussions require independent systems to create and disseminate knowledge and to scrutinise knowledge claims. Alongside universities and educational institutions, an independent news media is essential.

Here, I just make a formal point: news media cannot be understood in merely private terms. Broadcasting and organised journalism require corporate structures; corporate speech is not private speech; there must be legal obligations of truthfulness.

We know Kant as a rigorous advocate of truth-telling: virtue demands truth and truthfulness. As a matter of right, however, private speech may be 'true and sincere *or untrue and insincere* . . . for it is entirely up to [other people] whether they want to believe it or not' (6:238, my emphasis). We must not 'diminish' others' rights (6:238) – for example, by fraud (6:331) or slander (6:296 n, 466). But apart from this, private individuals have a *right to lie* (6:238).

This cannot apply to corporations. First, they must pursue publicly recognised purposes. As we have seen, individuals choose ends at their own discretion: each person must decide what to make of their life. Corporate purposes must be specified and justified. Second, if those purposes involve gaining and sharing knowledge, then untruth and insincerity betray this purpose, hence the basis for a corporation's very existence.

The only alternative would be to see news media as a source of entertainment. Kant knows that consumers may prefer comforting lies to hard truths (7:31, 8:436 f). Such preferences are a matter of virtue – or in this case, *vice*. Corporate purposes are a matter of right. Entertainment might have a place among them. But it cannot have priority over, or be allowed to undermine, essential elements of a rightful condition: that is, civic information and public reasoning.

Of course, this observation sets a problem rather than solving it: how to regulate news media while preserving their independence from government? (O'Neill 2013b, Klein 2015). Nonetheless, the point is pivotal to a Kantian framing. Corporations are artificial legal 'persons'. They are only justifiable if they serve justified purposes and do not corrupt essential public goods.

3.1.2 Democracy and Republicanism: 'Public Opinion' and Political Parties

Kant first approaches public right in terms of people's *possible* consent, as I discuss shortly (§3.3). But he also stresses the role of *actual* opinions:

> The estates of a knightly order can be revoked ... if public opinion has ceased to favour military honours as a means for safeguarding the state ... The holdings of the church can be similarly revoked if public opinion has ceased to want masses for souls, prayers and a multitude of clerics ... Those affected by such reforms cannot complain ... since the reason for their possession hitherto lay only in the *people's opinion* and also had to hold as long as that lasted. (6:324 f)

Since Kant also offers principled arguments against feudal arrangements and religious orthodoxy (§3.2.2, §3.3), we may wonder why 'public opinion' is so important here. Kant makes two points.

First, he says that states have a 'provisional right' to allow (for example) a hereditary nobility until 'public opinion' rejects their titles and privileges (6:329). This right may also be a duty. To avoid a state of nature, the civil state must be 'perpetual' (§2.3.2); people's rights may never be left hanging in midair. This duty to preserve the state is logically prior to 'great[er] conformity ... with principles of right' (6:318). To remain in existence, the state requires either oppression (contrary to right) or public acceptance. Public opinion *matters*.

Of course, Kant knows public opinion is hard to judge. Under non-democratic constitutions, the authorities decide what meets this test, just as they decide laws and policies.

This leads to the second point. Undemocratic arrangements do not fully conform to right. A 'true republic' is the only 'form of government suited to the idea of the original contract' (6:340; §2.4.1). In this case, the state really incorporates people as citizens. Under a 'representative system', citizens legislate 'by means of their delegates' (6:341; Kleingeld 2025). The republic not only upholds people's private rights and rightful honour – the essential condition of *permissible* willing. It also includes them as co-legislators – so that their willing is *actual*.

What does this mean for different types of corporation? – In general, equal freedom and rightful honour have strong implications for what sorts of corporation people and states *should* choose. But these principles also give weight to existing arrangements which are widely accepted. In this case, states have a 'provisional right' to let them continue (6:329). Citizens and their representatives can argue the case for change – or in other words, reason publicly. Democracies have broad powers to reform.

In addition, note that representative democracies rely on a type of corporation invented after Kant's death. *Political parties* first emerged as parliamentary groupings. Only in the nineteenth century did they become formal organisations beyond parliaments (Boix 2007).

We might argue whether parties are necessary for democracy – perhaps there are other ways of organising participation, representation and policy formation, waiting to be invented. Nonetheless, we know what a one-party state involves, and parties are central to representative democracies as we know them. For voters to choose, there must be competition between parties. More broadly, parties provide opportunities for debate, participation, and coalition-building across issues and sectors. As relatively stable corporate entities that aim to participate in government, they must craft coherent(ish!) policy programmes, in ways that social movements and single-issue groups need not.

3.1.3 Summary: Arguments from Public Right

Kant gives a principled argument for incorporation. Some tasks are essential to a rightful condition; they require long-term, collective action, but states should not undertake these tasks directly. On this basis, states should specifically charter some bodies. Kant's central example is universities – essential to the public use of reason. Legal frameworks should also give people civic rights people to incorporate for some purposes. The most important example, developed since Kant's death, are political parties – essential to representative democracy as we know it.

Corporations should also reflect public opinion. Kant offers principles to guide how people and states should judge. But these principles recognise the importance of actual opinions; democracy is the most rightful form of the state, because it incorporates those opinions.

Kant also suggests that some purposes are *useful* for a rightful condition. In particular, states might authorise corporations 'merely as means' (T&P 8:298) to security, stability, and prosperity. Kant's reference to 'prosperity' suggests that we apply this argument to business and trade. Section 4 considers this (§4.3).

In each case, corporations operate at arm's length from the state. They have their own purposes and powers, including the self-governing arrangements involved in their charters or constitutions. They must be open to reform, legal accountability and democratic oversight, in terms of these purposes, broader constitutional provisions, and (of course) how they exercise their legal powers. In §3.4.4, I return to the 'relative autonomy' of corporate bodies: 'arm's length' does not mean 'beyond reach'.

3.2 Ethics Requires Some Types of Corporation

Kant also suggests that incorporation may be justified in terms of private, virtuous purposes. This bridges his distinction between ethics and right.

3.2.1 Collective Virtue and 'Ethical Community'

Many virtuous ends can only be realised if people act together. In *Religion within the Boundaries of Mere Reason*, Kant offers an intriguing analogy. There can be an *ethical* state of nature, even after we have left the *juridical* one.

In a civil condition, we follow juridical laws; this grants us external freedom. This allows each person to 'prescribe the [ethical] law to himself'. So there may be 'no external [ethical] law to which he, along with others, acknowledges himself to be subject' (6:95).

This claim may sound strange, since Kant also insists that the Categorical Imperative is everyone's moral law. However, this imperative does not 'prescribe' specific forms of cooperation. (See also §4.2.1.) No one is bound to any specific ends or bound to act as means to those ends. For the most part, this is the picture we get from the *Metaphysics of Morals*. People still need to 'legislate' their social and ethical relations.

Religion therefore suggests that we 'may wish to enter with [our] fellow citizens into an ethical union over and above the political one' (6:95). This involves more than individual good will. It requires active cooperation and shared commitments. Beyond small and temporary groups, it requires a legal structure.

In this case, the state does not tell participants how to organise themselves or the specific purposes they should adopt. But it does provide legal terms for their association: *ethics incorporated*.

3.2.2 Religion, Charity, and the Government's 'Dignity'

Kant gives the example of churches. As corporations, they 'rest on public laws and have a constitution based on them' (6:96). But their concern is ethical, which must be separate from the state.

Kant writes that the government's dignity 'consists precisely in this: that it does not leave its subjects free to judge what is right or wrong according to their own notions, but [determines juridical right and wrong] for them by precepts of the legislative power' (7:25, see also 6:317 f). However, if the state tries to settle *non-juridical* rights and wrongs, it diminishes this dignity:

> For the supreme authority to say that a church should have a certain belief, or that it must maintain it unalterably and may not reform itself, are interferences which are *beneath its dignity*; for in doing this, as in meddling in the quarrels of the schools, it puts itself on a level of equality with its subjects ... (6:327)

As Kant puts it in 'What is Enlightenment?', if the state acts as priest, it 'exposes [it]self to the reproach *Caesar is not above the grammarians* ...' (8:41). Of course, the same applies if states try to judge questions of knowledge, not to mention grammar (§3.1.1).

By acting as if people were not entitled to decide these questions among themselves, the sovereign acts as 'one of the people' – as if its concerns and duties were the same as theirs. The state must not prescribe forms of religious worship. But it must provide a framework for religious congregation.

However otherworldly in spirit, religious practice requires worldly organisation: buildings, financial resources, officers, procedures to appoint and expel. Seen in this way, it is no coincidence that churches are among the oldest corporations. Already in 313, the Edict of Milan spoke of the 'Christian body corporate', including its right to own places of worship (Barker 1959: 470).

At the same time, Kant is cautious about religious corporations, for the same reason he opposes the narrow purpose and rigid structure of (supposedly) perpetual foundations (§2.3.1). Churches can enshrine hierarchy and orthodoxy, hindering possible progress:

> no people can ever decide to make no further progress in its insights regarding belief ... and so never to reform itself with regard to the church, since this

would be opposed to the humanity in their own persons. (6:327; also 8:38 f, 8:305)

People may agree to maintain the religious practices of their predecessors. But they cannot agree to be bound by these, simply as such. This would turn 'the humanity in their own persons' into mere means: by submitting to the dead, they give up their own responsibilities of judgement and their own rights of action. Bondage to the dead is the opposite of live consent.

In other words, when states give 'public laws' (6:96) to enable religious corporations, there is a double constraint: states should not dictate religious belief; they should not allow mere orthodoxy to gain legal force.

From a secular perspective, other types of corporation exemplify the same point: legal frameworks can enable virtuous activity; these frameworks must allow progress and intelligent response to changing circumstances.

Charities may pursue a range of beneficent purposes. Similarly, civic organisations can support social and political contributions. An old-fashioned English term, 'friendly societies', aptly describes organisations that provide mutual support and social insurance for members.

Again, these purposes require long-term organisation and dedicated resources. This means a legal framework, including procedures for owning, acquiring, and dispensing resources, and (re)apportioning responsibilities – or in other words, incorporation. This enables people to help one another anonymously, without risk of imposing on them (6:453). Organisations can act more impersonally, perhaps also more fairly, towards more people. As with religious bodies, the state cannot compel citizens to join in such virtuous purposes. But its legal frameworks play an essential facilitating role.

At the same time, caution is needed (§2.3.1). Some charitable foundations are unfair, wasteful and 'severely limit the freedom' of those they promise to help (6:367); founders may be motivated by vanity as well as virtue (6:369); purposes may become obsolete. As with religious bodies, these are not arguments against incorporating ethics. But whenever people draw on additional legal powers, it cannot be merely a matter of private judgement, whether these purposes merit support or should continue into an indefinite future. There must be oversight; reform must be possible.

3.2.3 Active Participation Requires Virtue, Too

Beyond specific ethical ends, corporations also require ethical commitment; decent corporations actively encourage this in their participants. Let me suggest some ways in which Kant's idea of ethical community bears on corporate organisation.

In any worthwhile organisation, many participants must show judgement and initiative. I have noted that people's motives may be mixed (§2.4.2): some employees may just want to 'do their jobs'; some members may just care about the benefits involved. Their conduct should contribute to the corporation's purpose, whatever their personal motives. However, that makes another sort of activity even more important. Some participants must actively shape the collective enterprise and its policies (Herzog 2018).

In one sense, corporate purposes are not matters of individual judgement. They are laid down in legal frameworks or a specific charter or the governing articles of the corporation. In another sense, participants *must* exercise judgement. Kypke's foundation offered a cautionary tale: purposes and structure must be open to revision. Perhaps the purpose or constitution could be better framed, or perhaps changing circumstances call for reform. At a more everyday level, purposes must be translated into ongoing policies and collective decisions; appropriate means must be found and deployed; cooperation always requires negotiation and compromise.

Notoriously, Kant says that 'a nation of devils' can behave rightfully, if given suitable laws – not least, threats of punishment (*PP* 8:366). Still, a republic requires many citizens who are committed to right. Otherwise democracy would be impossible. For example, Kant's devils would turn the public use of 'reason' into deceptive rationalising.

The same point applies to the corporate case with even greater force. Kant's devils must obey the law – mostly a matter of prohibitions (§2.1.1). Corporate participants must make active contributions, not just heed carrot and stick. When they act in terms of corporate purposes and policies, people make 'private use' of their reason (8:37). Here, 'private' means 'in the name of another' – in fact, in the name of an artificial person: church or state (8:38). Nonetheless, participants reason and judge. These are always *active* powers, for Kant.

This requires people who identify with their roles and the corporation and the purposes of both. Sometimes, it requires participants to look beyond – for example, to consider what role the corporation is playing as against other bodies, or what its external impacts are. In other words, at least some participants – and especially those empowered to shape policies and structures – must make the larger purpose part of their personal ends.

Kant's theory insists that law cannot require virtuous motivation, nor create it. It can only demand conduct that outwardly conforms to right, and punish conduct that does not. Nonetheless, a well-governed corporation can select, promote, and encourage participants who endorse its purposes and contribute to its integrity.

3.2.4 But Corporate Virtue Is Hard

We are familiar with corporate 'virtue signalling' and the cynicism that 'ethics talk' can invite. This should remind us of the sheer hard work in making corporations decent. It's bound to be hard, partly because there are so many obligations: to participants and employees, to clients or customers or patients, as well as to their own purposes and continuation.

It's also hard because a corporation, though a single body in law, is made up of many people. In any sizeable organisation, one department or policy does one thing; another department or policy does another. In other words, we can expect organisations to be confused, even hypocritical. This is not cynicism: it is built into the structure of large-scale collective action. Directors may assume they know what their organisation is doing; managers may assume that well-intentioned measures will generate intended results. Such assumptions make executives' lives easier, but they also encourage corporate vices: incoherence, negligence, wilful blindness, empty virtue signalling.

Corporate virtue requires many participants to be committed to intelligent, responsive pursuit of corporate purposes. It requires many participants to consider the wide range of obligations and activities involved in corporate agency. It requires self-knowledge – that is, reliable mechanisms to understand what the corporation's various parts are doing and what effects they are having. A decent organisation encourages these things, because it is cynical to take them for granted and naïve to ignore all the pressures that go in the opposite direction.

A Kantian framing offers no simple prescriptions, but it must insist on one point. Corporations must be governed; public right plays an essential role in setting the terms for this. In §4.4, I underline the special importance of knowledge, if participants are really to contribute to corporate purposes and integrity. Without a realistic picture of what the corporation is doing and achieving, participants can easily become *mere means* to unjust or unethical conduct.

3.3 Does 'Possible Consent' Support Laws of Incorporation?

Kant offers a well-known negative test for law-making: *could* a people agree? He puts the idea sharply: 'provided it is not self-contradictory that an entire people agree to such a law, however bitter they might find it, the law is in conformity with right' (T&P 8:299; compare 6:329, discussed in §3.1.2). This suggests that the state has broad powers to authorise corporations, even if people dislike them.

One problem with this suggestion is that it runs counter to the democratic aspects of Kant's thought – and ours. Another problem is that Kant himself sees this principle much more as a limit to corporate power. In his view, it is *impossible* for people to consent to some corporate purposes and structures.

However, the idea of possible consent is complicated. I will use it to highlight an important connection between right and virtue – and between wrong and vice. Corporate structures can undermine mutual respect and moral judgement.

3.3.1 Rightful Honour and Two Senses of Possible Consent

What is it possible for 'a people ... [to] decide with regard to itself' (6:329)? To answer this, we must distinguish 'can' (as a matter of fact) from 'may' (as a moral permission).

Shortly before he introduces innate right, Kant lays down the idea of *rightful honour*. Each person must 'assert [their] worth as a human being in relation to others, a duty expressed by the principle: "Do not make yourself a mere means for others but be at the same time an end for them"' (6:236). A person *can* violate this duty. Morally, they *may* not.

At first sight, this duty looks like a matter of ethics rather than right. In the *Doctrine of Virtue*, for example, Kant discusses the vice of servility. People *can* accept a subservient status, but they *may* not. Instead, they should adopt maxims such as '[D]o not be a parasite or a flatterer' and 'Be no man's lackey' (6:436).

Kant's word for 'lackey' is *Knecht* – the same word Hegel uses in his famous encounter of master and 'bondsman' (*Phenomenology of Spirit*, B.IV.A). The word can also refer to an inferior legal status.

This indicates why rightful honour is a duty of right as well as virtue. Kantian citizens must reject legal arrangements that go against this principle. No law may make some people mere means for others, or in other words, betray innate equality.

Although modern theorists of equality usually focus on the distribution of resources, inequality has often been a matter of corporate privilege. In Kant's time, these inequalities were ubiquitous: I have noted the French Revolution's hostility to corporations, as threatening equal freedom (§2.2.2). Feudal corporations often made some people into mere means for other people's ends.

3.3.2 Corporations That Undermine Rights Also Attack Virtue

Slavery is a legal status that makes a person into a mere means. It is fundamentally incompatible with rightful honour and innate right (Ripstein 2009: 135 ff, Pascoe 2022: §6). Some corporate structures created inherited statuses with similar effect. Kant draws no clear line between *Sklaven* and *Leibeigene*, a feudal term (6:241). *Leibeigene* were serfs or 'bondsmen': bound to a lord from birth, hence unfree. The structure was corporate. Landed estates and hereditary serfs were incorporated under an autocratic lord. The worst forms were utterly incompatible with Kantian principles.

Now consider a milder form, where the nobility has more limited rights. Rather than bondsmen, peasants live and work on their estates. Kant's condemnation is as blunt as any revolutionary's:

> an *hereditary* nobility is a rank that precedes merit and also provides no basis to hope for merit ... Since it cannot be accepted that any human being would throw away his freedom, it is impossible that the general will of the people would assent to such a groundless prerogative, hence also the sovereign cannot make it valid. (6:329; see also 8:433–6)

Kant does not call for immediate abolition, however, if 'public opinion' still accepts nobilities (6:329; see also *PP* 8:373 n; §3.1.2). However blunt, his criticism bears the ambiguity of possible consent ('cannot be accepted', 'impossible'). What people *can* (and do) accept is not always what they *may* (or should) accept.

One side of the problem concerns right. These legal arrangements undermine anyone who attempts to relate to others on a basis of mutual respect; they give legal support to everyone who does the opposite. This betrays innate equality and rightful honour.

The other side of the problem is ethical corruption (*Religion* 6:94, 97). As we have seen, rightful honour is inseparable from Kant's wider moral principles. Nobles expect peasants to act as mere means (6:450) and to 'think little of themselves in comparison with [them]' (6:465). Inherited titles and estates turn some people into 'parasites' and others into 'lackeys'; they encourage *vices* like arrogance and servility. If many people accept the senseless idea of inherited merit, then 'public opinion' is corrupted, too.[6]

In other words, the corrupt legal structure incorporates people in a concerted attack on Kantian principles. To overcome it, there must be change at two levels: broader moral attitudes *and* legal arrangements (§3.1.2, §3.2.4).

3.4 Freedom as a Justification for Incorporation (and a Limit Too)

As we have seen (§2.1), Kant describes property and contract as 'acquired rights'. He justifies them on the basis of a 'postulate of practical reason'. This invokes both our innate right to freedom and (of course) universal lawfulness. Since freedom often concerns association with others, we can extend this

---

[6] Corrupt public ideas about female and military honour also corrupt justice (6:335 ff; Timmermann 2024).

argument to rights of incorporation – just so long as this can be compatible with universal law and innate equality.

3.4.1 Justifying Acquired Rights

Here is Kant's opening claim:

> It is possible to have any external object of my choice as mine; i.e. a maxim by which, if it were to become law, an object of [possible] choice would ... become *ownerless* (*res nullius*) is contrary to right. (6:246)

To rephrase: legally, it is either permissible to use objects, or it is not. To make it illegal would be like putting a glass wall between ourselves and the world. Things, spaces, even other people's actions would be unusable. This would be 'contrary to right', as Kant now explains:

> For an object of my choice is something that I *physically* have the power to use. However, should it completely be outside my power *juridically* to make use of this object, i.e. should [such use] not be able to coexist with the freedom of everyone in accordance with a universal law ... then freedom would be depriving itself of the use of its faculty of choice with regard to an object of [possible] choice, by putting *usable* objects beyond any possibility of *use*; i.e. it would annihilate them in a practical respect and make them into *res nullius*, even though choice in the use of things is formally consistent with everyone's external freedom in accordance with universal laws. (6:246)

So long as it is compatible with freedom under universal law, things ('*res*') cannot be nothing ('*nullius*') to us. For any object of choice, practical reason 'postulates' or 'presupposes' (6:246) a possible legal relation.

Kant starts with people's '*physical* ... power to use' things and spaces. The first sort of acquired right is property. As a matter of universal law, it is possible for *one* person to own *some* things, compatibly with *everyone else*'s rights to own *countless other* things. Our holdings are bound to be different and unequal in countless ways, but formally, we are equal rights-holders.

Contract is more complex. Normally, I do not have the 'physical power' to use someone else's actions. But contract enables people to commit specific actions to one another. I acquire the right that you deliver me a cake next week; you acquire the right to my paying. Again, this is compatible with *everyone else* having rights to make contracts over *countless other* actions. Despite people's differing contractual commitments, they remain formally equal.

These examples only scratch the surface. Here are two from public right.

Unless there were public highways, people would be confined to their respective private spaces. Granted a system of private dwellings, there must also be public spaces that allow everyone to reach other private spaces (Ripstein

2009: Ch. 8). Otherwise, people could only travel and associate with others if intervening neighbours permitted them. Everyone would be bound by others – a condition of equal *un*freedom; the opposite of Kantian equal freedom. So the state must create public rights of way. Further laws regulate people's uses of these public 'objects of choice', to make sure all members of the public (§1.3.3) enjoy the same right: to move and to associate with others in a given territory.

Or consider a nature reserve that no one may enter. This may seem like non-use, even *res nullius*. Formally, however, it is another type of use: it preserves natural resources for future generations. Law creates a collective 'object of choice' by prohibiting normal use.

In other words, Kant's abstract framing quickly takes us beyond the individual, physical case. It is obvious that we cannot conceive, never mind will, a world where we do not use things and spaces. Kant does not even mention this. Instead, he focuses on freedom. *Choice* includes duty and wish as well as need. Of course, there is no freedom if people die of hunger or confinement. But free people can do much more than meet their needs. Not least, they can create entirely new 'objects of [possible] choice' – between two people in private contract; between everyone in the case of public highways; between generations in the case of nature reserves.

3.4.2 How Does This Apply to Incorporation?

Human beings have learned to achieve many purposes through the corporate form – from its beginnings in Roman law, through feudal arrangements for church and society, into modern times. As we have seen, corporations are artificial legal 'persons'. They have defined purposes, changing membership, intelligent governance structures. Although some types of corporation enable immoral purposes, others are essential to right or ethically important.

This opens a whole new field of 'objects of choice' – that is, means by which people can achieve their ends. So Kant's 'postulate' has an important implication. Freedom demands that we create legal frameworks for these. 'Objects of choice' should not stand beyond the possibility of use. In the name of freedom, people should have rights to combine with others to achieve worthwhile purposes.

To be clear, this is not a right to other people's cooperation: that would limit *their* freedom. Nor is it a right to freedom of association: this is already implied by innate right (§2.1, §2.2.4). Instead, incorporation enables people to take part in specified forms of cooperation, using dedicated resources, without depending on any specific person.

But then note the Kantian proviso. These 'objects' must be compatible with innate equality and freedom under universal law.

3.4.3 Two Formal Points about Universal Law, with Huge Material Implications

We can see how demanding this proviso is by considering, first, people's legal capacities within corporations, and second, corporations' legal powers to act in the world.

Section 2 already insisted that the first point is central to a Kantian approach. When someone acts for a corporation, they gain power and lose legal responsibility (§2.2.2). They might use corporate powers and resources as mere means to their private ends, without corresponding liability. This would be contrary to innate equality: each person's 'independence from being bound by others to more than one can in turn bind them' (6:237).

This risk exists just so long as a person acts on behalf of an artificial person. It does not matter how equitable or democratic the corporation is, or even its scale and resources. Nonetheless, size and hierarchy increase the material dangers. There are greater powers to act. Internal accountability is harder. Higher-ups can decide where benefits fall – and costs too. Their missteps may cost other participants dearly, sometimes outsiders too.

Then a second point. A new legal person poses new risks of wrongs – for both participants and outsiders. But our familiar legal and ethical safeguards do not apply. An old complaint highlights the basic problem: 'Did you ever expect a corporation to have a conscience, when it has no soul to be damned, and no body to be kicked?'[7]

Compare the birth of a human being. As someone grows up, they gain the physical abilities and legal capacity to wrong other people. Law and conscience provide only fallible safeguards. But a person is an end in themselves: everyone must honour their in-born right to live and act on terms of equal freedom. For corporate persons, there is no such 'must'. And the familiar safeguards are much more fallible. These formal points gain huge material significance, the larger and more powerful a corporation becomes.

We have seen the point about corporations having 'no body to kick' (§2.2.1). There is no natural person to punish, unless one or a few participants are clearly responsible for the corporate wrong. This is always hard to demonstrate, especially in a large organisation. More broadly, there are no unambiguous penalties by which to deter or punish a corporate 'body'.

---

[7] Attributed to Edward, First Baron Thurlow (1731–1806); discussed in Coffee Jr 1981.

What about 'no soul'? As private individuals, we are guided by principles of virtue, and perhaps by fear of punishment. A corporation is not. It has a specific purpose and a decision-making structure. Its participants are meant to act in terms of these. Of course, participants should not abandon conscience (8:38) or 'inner morality' (6:371; §4.2.1). But they share responsibility for a corporate whole. The whole becomes harder to see and to steer, the more powerful it becomes (§3.2.4, §4.4.4).

This matters, because corporations can commit most of the wrongs that people can, and more besides. For example, Kant mentions an inquisitor (6:186 f). The official agent of a religious corporation (§2.2.2) perpetrates the very worst bodily crimes.

Then there are wrongs that only corporations can commit, or at least, are far better equipped to. For example, the English East India Company was notorious for corrupting Parliamentary decisions (§4.3); large organisations can pollute at scales beyond any individual. Specific corporate powers make new abuses possible: think of a political party's power to campaign in elections, or a trade union's power to call strike action. The larger a corporation, the greater the dangers.

Again, we can frame the issue in terms of possible consent. On what conditions can people consent to the 'birth' of a corporation – a potential wrong-doer whose wrongs law must struggle to deter or punish? At a minimum, public right must structure and oversee the corporation to limit the risks of wrongdoing.

Both the formal features of collective action and hard experience suggest that 'corporate conscience' is hard. It requires care in defining purposes and structures; caution in selecting appropriate participants (especially those with significant responsibilities); vigilance for early signs that things may be going awry; mechanisms to gather and generate knowledge about corporate activities and impacts (§4.4.4).

In sum, freedom under universal law demands much more than individual rights not to participate. There must be mechanisms to guard against private abuse. There must be ways to prevent and pre-empt corporate wrongdoing. All citizens deserve safeguards against these dangers: nothing else is compatible with freedom and equality, rightful honour or possible consent.

3.4.4 Policing, Policy, and Regulation

Occasionally, Kant can sound like Adam Smith in his warnings about state intervention. For example, Kant tells the story of a government minister who asked merchants 'for suggestions on how to stimulate trade – as if he would know how to choose the best of these'.

Kant seems to have his own view about the best, however. He quotes one merchant: 'Build good roads, mint sound money, give us laws for exchanging money ... but as for the rest, leave us alone!' He suggests this should apply to government policies for universities: 'just don't interfere with the progress of understanding and science' (7:20 n).

But let me take a caution from Adam Smith. If the merchants had demanded rights to incorporate, he would warn us to expect a conspiracy against the public – in other words, the opposite of free trade (Muthu 2008). Kant is less concerned with economic life (more in Section 4). But we have seen his cautions about unjust corporations (§2.3.1, §3.3); states must have wide powers to reform. In addition, states have duties to oversee and regulate. Kant calls this a '*Recht der Polizei*' (6:327).

To translate this as 'right of police' would not capture Kant's meaning. This is closer to what we now call 'public policy': regulation and oversight to secure order and welfare. This includes rules governing markets (6:303), 'public security, convenience and decency' (6:325), as well as the state's right to 'inspect' associations that might affect 'public well-being' (6:325). (For discussion, see Stewart 2014.)

This is a significant power, and it can easily overstep the mark. This is the lesson Kant draws from the merchants. He offers the same caution with regard to churches:

> A state has only a *negative* right to prevent public teachers [priests] from exercising an influence ... detrimental to public peace. Its right is therefore that of policing. (6:327; likewise *Religion* 6:96)

In other words, Kant's view acknowledges two threats. States can demand too much control over corporations. But corporations can also undermine public right and public goods. In Hobbes's famous phrase, corporations may resemble 'many lesser Commonwealths in the bowels of a greater, like worms in the entrails of a natural man' (*Leviathan*, Ch. XXIX) – parasites that damage the health of the body politic.

Like Hobbes's sovereign, dictators want every organisation to lie in their grasp. They claim rights to seize corporate assets, to sack or appoint or intimidate officers, to dictate or overturn day-to-day decisions, and so on. Kant rejects this. Whether political parties or universities, charities or churches, corporations should exercise their powers with 'a certain autonomy' (7:17).

But corporations can act like small versions of Hobbes's sovereign. They may not claim a dictator's sweeping powers, but they still claim freedom from accountability and regulation. Feudal lords, inquisitorial priests, the barons of big tech or polluting industries: in different ways, all want to act beyond the reach of state law, public policy, or democratic controls.

Again, Kant rejects this. The 'right of policy' applies with special force wherever states grant powers and authorise privileges. This happens with every corporation: people gain additional powers to act, over and above their rights as private individuals. The point has even more weight when corporations are large or exercise special powers.

Seen in this way, rule-governed oversight and democratically sanctioned regulations are not arbitrary interferences: they are fundamental requirements. Innate equality and possible consent demand measures to ensure that corporations do not undermine rights, corrupt ethics, or tend towards wrongdoing.

The details are bound to be difficult, requiring democratic debate and 'judgement sharpened by experience' (4:389). But the overarching point is simple. 'Arm's length' is not 'beyond reach'. A corporation exists by a grant of artificial legal personality; this empowers some people to act beyond their private rights. 'Policing' corporate activity is quite different from regulating people's private conduct. It is also indispensable.

Conclusion to Section 3

Section 2 argued that a corporation must have *some* specified purpose. Otherwise it simply extends some people's private agency. That would betray rightful equality.

This section has shown how Kant justifies a range of purposes. Universities and news media allow the organised pursuit and sharing of knowledge. Religious bodies and charities pursue ethical goals. Each case demands incorporation.

We now know many more corporate purposes; most likely, there are other possibilities waiting to be invented. Business corporations were just emerging in Kant's time (Section 4); they can take many forms (§4.1.6), not least because business does not involve a single purpose (§4.3). Political parties are arguably the most important type of corporation devised since Kant's death (§3.1.2), central to democratic representation as we know it. I have bracketed international and transnational corporations (§1.3.4); many forms have emerged since Kant wrote. Although Kant's theory provides a valuable framework, I do not think it can anticipate the many corporate forms that might be apt to different circumstances. This is a field for civic creativity rather than a priori ordering.

Diverse as they are bound to be, corporations always combine public authority with private initiative. Even to exist, they rely on some grant of public power; they may also exercise specific privileges – for example, to grant degrees or to broadcast. At the same time, they depend on citizens' willingness to take part. They bridge Kant's distinction between public and private right.

In different ways, corporations also bridge Kant's distinction between right and virtue. Positively, some types of corporation pursue virtuous ends. A charity must provide public benefit, for example. In this case, law enables long-term, collective, *ethical* action. In this sense, right cannot be neutral between ethical purposes and self-serving or vicious ones. But granting citizens the right to found and run a charity leaves much room for judgement and initiative. Which public benefits do they see as worth pursuing or supporting?

In addition, sustaining a decent corporation demands virtue. In §§3.2.3–4, I briefly raised some points that go beyond Kant's own words. Some corporate structures foster decent conduct and the sharing of moral purposes. In the worst cases, corporations encourage vice. Feudal hierarchies did this. Both libertarian and republican authors criticise hierarchical employment for similar effects (e.g. Cornuelle 1991, Anderson 2017); I will raise a related criticism in the next section (§4.4).

More broadly, body-less, soul-less corporations pose moral problems and make moral demands that cut across Kant's right-virtue distinction. These have become hugely significant for modern societies. It is hard to deter and punish wrongs. So pre-empting wrongdoing takes on a special urgency. As well as 'policing' or regulatory policy, this requires the corporate equivalent of virtue.

The most basic precondition for this is *knowledge*. Both for insiders and outsiders, it is hard to know what a corporation is really doing. Collective action already poses difficulties. Hierarchy can make it easier for a collective to act 'as one', but it also cuts against shared knowledge.

Beyond the obvious dangers of negligent or reckless corporate activity, ignorance is incompatible with the condition needed to prevent a corporation from merely extending a private person's agency. A corporation must pursue its own defined purposes, intelligently and responsively. When public right authorises incorporation, it must also insist on measures to show whether a corporation is doing this. All experience teaches us that this is hard: it requires internal structures to create and share knowledge, as well as external reporting and oversight.

With these cautions in mind, Section 4 turns to corporations that might be means to promote a rightful condition. Kant mentions prosperity as one way to promote right (§3.1.3). This brings us to our world's dominant type of corporation: business.

Appendix to Section 3: Hegel's Corporation

Hegel's *Philosophy of Right* (1821) remains a landmark response to Kant's practical philosophy. Famously, it argues that corporations should play an important social and civic role (§§250–6). How does this compare with Kant's approach?

At an abstract level, the two accounts are parallel. Corporations sit between individual and state. Corporations should develop people's capacities to act and reason with others, in ways that serve valuable ends. Like Kant, Hegel recognises the importance of religious bodies (§270 R). He also mentions charitable foundations (§§242, 245). Both authors stress the state's duty to oversee or 'police', alongside corporations' self-governing aspects.

Hegel's view is famous partly because, unlike Kant, he underlines the importance of 'civil society' between individual and state. In his view, this sphere helps people develop a concrete sense of their individual duties. It recognises people as actual participants and contributors, rather than abstract individuals (§253; see §1.4).

Hegel's view is also famous because he proposes a specific type of corporation. This has no parallel in Kant and it has never been realised in practice. Each trade and profession, Hegel suggests, should have a corporation that unites its practitioners (§§251–2).

In some respects, these proposed corporations resemble medieval guilds. Members regulate their practices within a collective body – for example, by developing shared skills and enforceable standards for their work (§254). Unlike the feudal bodies, however, membership should be voluntary; it may be limited, but not closed or hereditary.

In addition, Hegel envisaged these corporations as enabling solidarity – for example, they would organise mutual insurance to help members who suffer misfortune (§253 R). Corporations would also play a broader political role – members would elect representatives to participate in political decision-making (§§308–11).

As this implies, Hegel does not share Kant's fundamental concern with equality. Social and political order rest on differences in 'estate'; his corporations give civic expression to these inequalities. In addition, Hegel's proposal fitted badly with the new order emerging before his eyes – above all, the increasing scale, complexity, and dynamism of modern economies. Some of the purposes he envisaged have since been served by trade unions, mutual and friendly societies, professional associations, trade bodies, and cooperatives, at least in some sectors. But these bodies have never played the systematic social and political role that Hegel had in mind.

Not least, Hegel's proposal bears no resemblance to the type of corporation that dominates contemporary life: the business corporation (Klikauer 2016). This is our topic in Section 4.

4 Incorporating Business

This section offers a Kantian view of the business corporation, and especially its most common form: a corporation with shareholders. Kant said relatively little about business. Modern Kantians have also said little, apart from some contributions to business ethics. So this section is more exploratory.

The first part gives some historical background. I note Kant's comments about early business corporations and his own shareholding. I then sketch how these early corporations laid the ground for modern, shareholder-based business corporations. I also note some alternative forms.

The second part emphasises the structure of Kant's moral theory. Before we explore questions of virtue, we must consider legal structures. We cannot move directly from the Categorical Imperative or abstract Kantian principles to conclusions about the duties of directors or employees. Legal powers to incorporate provide the basis for these duties.

The third part considers justifications for business incorporation. The arguments are less straightforward than those considered in Section 3. Business involves a range of activities, all essential if companies are to compete successfully. There is no point in law requiring companies to pursue purposes that are already essential to them. But the formal Kantian condition still applies: incorporation cannot be merely a means for some people to pursue their private purposes. I argue for a broader, public justification: *prosperity that supports rightful conditions*.

Finally, I turn to employees. They are means to corporate ends: are they mere means? One set of worries concerns exploitation: are workers employed on fair terms, with reasonable options? A second set of problems is less noticed. Can employees know whether they are means to immorality? I suggest that current laws pose a serious challenge. Workers must do as they are told in large, secretive hierarchies. By 'just following orders', they may act as instruments of harm, not agents of prosperity.

4.0.1 A Note on Terminology and Focus

For simplicity, this section focuses on business within a single jurisdiction, with just a brief note on transnational corporations (§4.1.5).

For brevity, *companies law* refers to the legal frameworks that authorise *business corporations* or simply *companies*. I will assume that these companies have *shareholders* and that shares are traded on public stock exchanges. But there are also privately held corporations (with a small group of shareholders), and several other alternatives (§4.1.6).

I also set aside some complexities in corporate governance. Shareholder rights are a complex bundle that varies between jurisdictions and even within the same corporation: for example, there may be 'non-voting shares'; large shareholders sometimes have duties as well as rights. In a few jurisdictions, companies must involve worker representatives in their governance – thus 'co-determination' in Germany. (See Kraakman et al. 2017 on all these aspects.) For simplicity, I refer to all senior figures as *directors*, including executives and senior managers appointed by the legal directors.

4.1 Some History

Nowadays, we often use the word 'corporation' to mean a business organisation. This is a recent development. Before the seventeenth century, corporations sometimes organised forms of trade. But these bodies – guilds and regulated companies – did not do business in their own right. Only in the nineteenth century was business routinely incorporated.

4.1.1 State-Sponsored 'Trading Companies', Including the East India Companies

Kant knew about the first business corporations: 'trading companies' chartered by 'commercial states'. The Dutch and English East India Companies are the most famous examples, both founded at the beginning of the seventeenth century (§2.2.2, §2.5.1). Kant's only published comment is damning:

> the inhospitable behaviour of civilized, especially commercial, states in our part of the world, the injustice they show in visiting foreign lands and peoples (which with them is tantamount to conquering them) goes to horrifying lengths ... the commercial states do not even profit from this violence ... all these trading companies are on the verge of collapse ... the Sugar Islands, that place of the cruellest and most calculated slavery, yield no true profit but serve only a mediate and indeed not very laudable purpose, namely, training sailors for warships and so, in turn, carrying on wars in Europe, and this for [states] that make much ado of their piety and ... drink wrongfulness like water ... (*PP* 8:358 f; see also 6:353)

These state-sponsored corporations were as much colonial as commercial. They represented one of the main ways in which people breached Kant's innovative category of cosmopolitan right: the relation between 'visitors' and 'foreign lands and peoples'.

Kant alleges that this 'trading' was unprofitable. Admittedly, systematic corruption bankrupted the Dutch Company just as Kant was writing the words above. But both the Dutch and English Companies brought enormous wealth to their home countries.

The Companies have another claim to fame. They pioneered the legal structure that dominates modern economies: business corporations with publicly traded shares. This structure combines: directors (who govern the corporation); shareholders (who buy shares in the hope of gain); employees (who work for pay); and a permanent 'stock' of productive assets.

Before this, 'joint stock' was a tool for time-limited merchant ventures. For example, merchants might join forces to buy and stock a ship (§2.1.2). The merchants 'unjoined' their stock when the ship returned, hopefully recouping their original investment and a share of profits.

As Kant hints, colonising ventures do not yield quick profits. They require long-term investment in ships, weapons, military outposts, and more. A permanent corporation made more sense.

The Dutch Company led the way, in three respects. First, it involved joint stock from the start. Second, it took money from many more people – all residents of the Netherlands could become stockholders (*Octrooi VOC 1602*: Art. X). Third, the merchant-directors (§2.2.2) and political authorities made it into a permanent corporation decades before the English one.

This corporate transformation led to widespread protests (Ciepley 2023: 860 f). On the original agreement, the stockholders would regain their share of the stock after ten years. Now the stock became the Company's, permanently. The original stockholders became mere stock-certificate-holders, or as we now say, *shareholders*.

4.1.2 The Birth of Shareholder Rights

The Dutch shareholders were bought off with two rights; the English Company involved a third. These rights proved very lucrative. They laid down the structure of modern capitalism: directors and shareholders govern business corporations, which in turn govern employees.

The first right was to a share in dividends, instead of a redistribution of stock plus profits at the end of the venture. Corporate directors can pay some profits out as dividends, in proportion to shareholdings. Directors can also retain profits at their discretion – this enables corporations to invest and grow in perpetuity.

Second was the right to sell stock certificates to any buyer. This gave rise to modern stock exchanges. This created another way for shareholders to gain.

Certificates might trade for more (often much more) than their initial value, especially if the company is profitable or growing.

A third right was largely absent in the Dutch Company, but more central to the English. Shareholders could participate in corporate governance, receiving information and voting in the election of corporate directors. This right has varied a lot – between jurisdictions and even within the same corporation. Historically, it sometimes worked on a 'one member, one vote' principle (thus the earlier stages of the English Company). This model disappeared a long time ago. Now, voting rights reflect the number of shares you own. If you own many shares, you gain real power.

A historical side-note. Prussia chartered its first share-based businesses in 1770 and 1782: sugar refineries in Breslau and Königsberg (Thieme 1960: 292). At his death, Kant left a considerable shareholding in the Königsberg refinery (Bundeskunsthalle 2023: *Koloniale Verstrickungen*). This sugar was hardly innocent: it came from colonial ventures that Kant himself condemned.

4.1.3 The Birth of Routine Business Incorporation

The colonial 'trading companies' and Prussian sugar refineries rested on state charters (§2.5.1). These were fairly rare. Elizabeth I, for example, took a lot of persuading to charter the English East India Company. What did the state stand to gain?

For merchants and businessmen, the advantages were clearer. I have mentioned problems of joint property (§2.1; also 6:234). This is related to another problem: if you do business in your own name, as partners do, you risk everything. But if you direct a corporation, there is no risk to your personal property (§2.2.2). This is what artificial legal personhood means: the corporation owns property (and debts!), not individuals; the corporation acts, rather than the people who make its decisions; the corporation can be immortal, independent of any natural person.

Hoping for such advantages, businessmen made persistent legal efforts to mimic the corporate form. These led to the 'joint stock company', crucial to Britain's economic life in the eighteenth and nineteenth centuries. Since private rights are not enough to create a distinct legal person, a lot of legal ingenuity was involved, along with some complicity from the legal system. The result was messy; recourse to law was costly and uncertain (Harris 2000: Ch. 6). Here I just want to stress two larger points.

First, these companies again involved shareholders and directors (or trustees, acting 'in trust' for holders of the 'joint stock'). Directors governed the company on a day-to-day basis. At least in theory, they answered to shareholders, usually at annual meetings. Second, these companies showed the importance of legal frameworks for business. Even in its early, uncertain forms, the joint stock company could support growing economic activity.

European and North American states took notice. From the mid nineteenth century, they passed laws that enabled people to create a business corporation by following some routine procedures (§2.5.2). Directors could invest their own money in it, in return for shares. Or they could persuade others to buy shares, on the basis of their business proposals and the security offered by legal frameworks.

This shift makes it easy to think of modern business corporations as private. They command no state-sponsored monopoly; they have no state-sponsored mission; they require no specific charter. Nonetheless, they still require state authorisation to exist and to act. In the terms I have used here (§1.3.3, §2.5.2): when people draw on this authorisation, they exercise a civic right, not a private one.

4.1.4 Shareholders Own Shares; They Do Not Own the Corporation

The language of 'shares' invites confusion. It is natural to suppose that 'shareholders' own a share *of the corporation*. But on a Kantian view – and arguably, on any accurate view of the law (Ciepley 2013) – this is impossible.

Simply, an artificial person is not the sort of thing that can be owned. Property rights relate to *things*: 'mere means', on Kant's view. It is impossible to own people, not even people considered in their corporate roles. If people are to be 'bound', this requires a different legal form (§2.4, §4.4). An artificial legal person is a legal actor with its own rights, duties, and participants. It must be *governed*. But governing is conceptually distinct from ownership.

This is obvious for the types of corporation discussed in Section 3. People govern charities or universities, for example. But no one owns them, neither state nor office-holders nor members.

The point is harder to see in the business case, because shareholding is such a peculiar institution. Unlike other corporations, people can buy and sell rights to participate in governing – the second and third rights noted earlier (§4.1.2). How does this tradeable right to part-govern differ from part-ownership?

We already saw part of the answer. In the case of partnership, partners may jointly own assets – a ship and its stock, for example (§2.1.2). By contrast, each East India Company owned *its own* ships and stock. Hence the protests of Dutch shareholders (§4.1.1): they no longer owned ships or stock – just stock certificates, with their peculiar bundle of rights.

The difference from joint ownership gets clearer if we consider the other side of the coin: the duties that go with rights. As well as assets and profits, partners own any *debts* they incur when they do business. They are personally liable – to their 'last shilling and acre', in the old legal phrase. Compare the risk faced by merchants in the early stages of the Dutch East India Company (§2.2.2).

If shareholders were owners, they would own company debts. If the company lacked funds, they would be obliged to pay its damages, too. But shareholders have no such obligations. This is what it means, for the company to be a legal person: it has its own rights and duties, including liability for its own debts and wrongs. Shareholders help govern this artificial person, and have some rights to benefit from it. But they are not liable for its actions.

From the point of view of Kantian innate equality, this has the air of scandal (§2.2.2). For Kant, unequal holdings of property do not alter people's formal equality as right-and-duty-bearers (with caveats: §4.4.3). But shareholding involves a distinct form of right. Wealthier people buy the right to act through an additional legal person, and to benefit if it does well. They have no duties to meet that 'person's' debts or to compensate its wrongs.

4.1.5 Two Further, World-Changing Historical Facts

Laws for routine business incorporation also included a new power. They allowed companies themselves to own shares. As such, one corporation could become the exclusive or majority shareholder of another. As just stressed, this does not mean *owning* the other corporation; but it does mean rights to govern, by appointing directors. Mergers and takeovers followed. This helped some corporations assume enormous size.

Second, Western states exported these laws, as Katharina Pistor and colleagues note:

> The majority of countries around the globe copied or received the foundations of their corporate law from ... France, England and Germany, as a result of colonization, legal imposition after a lost war, or as a result of (semi-) voluntary subjugation to foreign pressure ... (Pistor et al. 2002: 799 f)

These two facts provide the basis for modern transnationals. The East India Companies mostly crossed borders by violent conquest. A modern transnational corporation (TNC) works differently.

In law, a TNC is not a single body. Rather, it is a network with a centralised control structure. There is a parent corporation, headquartered in a specific state. This corporation owns the shares of subsidiary corporations abroad. Hence it can appoint their directors and govern their operations. The TNC's reach may be global.

Despite the importance of TNCs, the rest of this section focuses on business corporations within a single jurisdiction. A Kantian framing of transnational structures first requires us to analyse the simpler case. This is already no easy task.

4.1.6 Alternative Forms of Business Corporation

The shareholder-based business corporation and its networked cousin, the transnational corporation, dominate modern economies. But there are other ways of incorporating business.

A trust corporation is a business with shares. But the shares are owned by a charitable trust, which then has the further purpose of making grants for public benefit. Cooperatives and 'worker-owned' businesses are also types of corporation. There are non-profit business corporations. In some jurisdictions, 'benefit corporations' specify social benefits as part of their purpose.

In what follows, I set these possibilities to one side, because they are much less important economically. Morally, however, they matter enormously. I believe that Kantians should have deep reservations about the shareholder-based corporation. But this does not mean they should reject legal frameworks for business. There are many alternative possibilities that may avoid or lessen the problems I raise in the rest of this section.

4.2 Kant's Approach: Morality, Right, Ethics

Some influential contributions to business ethics take an explicitly Kantian perspective (e.g. White 2011, Bowie 2017). There is much to learn from this literature, but it also calls for caution. Too often, it misses the guiding method of Kant's moral theory.

This is not just a problem with Kantian approaches. Wider debates about business often miss or mistake how business corporations rest on political decisions. So we talk about markets and regulation in misleading ways.

4.2.1 Law Shapes Individuals' Powers and Obligations

In the *Groundwork*, Kant sets out the basic principle of morality: the famous Categorical Imperative. Many readers assume we can use it to derive our everyday obligations. For example, one version of the Categorical Imperative says we must 'use humanity ... always at the same time as an end, never merely as a means' (4:429). Principles of honesty and non-instrumentalisation seem to follow directly. Kant's own examples suggest that these abstract moral principles translate smoothly into individual duties.

In this case, it seems natural to suppose that corporate managers and executives bear the same duties. We just need to work out how they apply to specific issues, like sweatshop labour (Preiss 2014) or lobbying and tax avoidance (Van de Vijver 2022).

However, Kant's own method is more complex. He starts by laying the ground abstractly: the Categorical Imperative is like an overarching *constitution* for morality. (Kant's word is *Grundgesetz*, an explicitly political analogy: 5:30 f; Kleingeld 2018: 166 f.) To give an account of individual duties, Kant then moves to questions of right. Questions of virtue follow (§1.3). In other words, we must know our legal rights and duties in order to make individual ethical decisions.

To take a simple example: as an abstract moral principle, we should help other people (4:423). But what we can do to help depends on our rights. I can use my property to help you. Except in emergency, I can't use someone else's property to do so. However well-intentioned, that would be theft.

In a more complex way, this point applies to people's duties within corporations. For example, a charity trustee has duties to pursue the charity's specified public benefits (§2.4.2). The trustee may believe that another cause is more deserving. But they cannot use the charity's resources to address it. However well-intentioned, that would be misappropriation.

In other words, the legal structure requires officers and members and employees to act in 'in the name of another' (§3.2.3) – in the name of the corporation, that is. They draw on corporate powers and resources; they are subject to corporate policies, goals, and purposes. They may not use the corporation as a mere means to enhance their private powers of action. Instead, their duties and powers are largely given by their role and the legal structure in which it sits. We need to understand these, if moral reflection is to move beyond abstract principles.

Let me add a vital qualification: Kant's stress on legal rights and duties is not a demand for 'just following orders'. Morality is always the *Grundgesetz* or 'grounding law'. Kant emphasises that an office-holder 'would have to resign' if asked to act against 'inner morality' ('What Is Enlightenment?' 8:38, 6:371). In modern contexts, and especially where damaging information is being hidden (§4.4.4), we may also think of duties to report or 'blow the whistle'.

But then note the coercive and collective faces of law. Corporate structures are backed by law. Where these structures attack morality (§3.3.2), individuals face very hard choices. Law entitles other people to insist on your corporate duties. When conscience insists that you must reject those duties, the personal costs can be immense.

4.2.2 A Parallel Point Applies to 'Corporate Social Responsibilities'

The basic problem starts with the sequence just mentioned: morality, right, ethics. This applies to artificial persons even more than natural persons. Law must grant rights to all human beings: it exists to uphold people's equal freedom. For Kant, this freedom is ultimately in the service of our moral agency. As such, Kant does not hesitate to speak of 'natural right' (e.g. 6:237 f). Likewise, he speaks of parents' 'natural duty' towards their children (6:330).

But an artificial person only exists 'in contemplation of law' (§1.1). Nothing depends on nature. Everything depends on the rights, purposes, and powers that law grants.

Of course, it still makes sense to discuss the duties of corporations, in ways that go beyond the narrowly legalistic. They are human creations, created and sustained for human purposes. As the central example for this section, consider the idea of corporate social responsibility.

Like individuals, corporations surely have duties to respect public goods and people, to plan ahead and with knowledge of what they are doing. It is 'socially irresponsible' to pollute, exploit, ignore the long-term, or close your eyes to the impacts of your own conduct. Roughly speaking, these are the corporate equivalent of personal immorality. Pollution vandalises public goods. Exploitation is a type of instrumentalisation (§4.4.3). Short-termism and wilful blindness are serious forms of irresponsibility (Heffernan 2011; §4.4.4).

In general terms, Kantians cannot deny these responsibilities. To specify them more closely is a large task; discussions of corporate social responsibility make vital contributions to public reasoning about them. Here, I want to stress why this reasoning is difficult.

To illustrate, consider a market sector where many businesses use low-ranking workers as mere means. Workplace injuries are common and breadline wages are standard, for example. Abstract Kantian principles certainly apply; we know that *something* is wrong. However, it is rarely clear who is *doing* wrong. Most likely, the problem is not that a few managers have failed to appreciate their duty to treat employees as ends-in-themselves. The problem is more complex – or as we might say, more *corporate*. Even business directors might be unable to overcome the problems, given their other legal obligations and the competitive context in which their businesses act.

Compare hereditary nobilities, mentioned earlier (§3.3.2). No doubt, there are individual vices at work. But the first culprit, so to speak, is a legal structure which attacks Kantian morality. I suggest a parallel analysis applies here. If we observe widespread exploitation, then we may criticise the people involved. But we must also consider the legal basis – the structure and duties and 'powers to bind' created by incorporation. Does this honour people's equality and other core Kantian principles? Or does it promote immorality and irresponsibility?

4.2.3 A Reminder: Corporations Do Not Arise from Private Right

In contrast to the types of corporation discussed in Section 3, we often assume that business corporations do not require legal authorisation. This deepens the problem just mentioned. Public debates rarely acknowledge that business corporations depend on state authorisation. So they ignore how public right may authorise and encourage social irresponsibility.

On one influential view, the company is just a 'nexus of contracts' (Easterbrook & Fischel 1989). This view does not deny that companies law *exists*. But this law just makes it easier for people to do what they already could, by exercising their private rights to property and contract.

Seen in this way, business corporations represent a compromise between people's private ends. For example: employees want paid work; customers want goods or services; directors want pay or perks or power; lenders want repaying; shareholders want financial gains. If this were true, then laws to structure or regulate business corporations would *limit freedom*. They would interfere in people's right to strike their own bargains – including 'corporate contracts' (§2.4.6).

Easterbrook and Fischel were enthusiasts for the supposedly private business corporation. Critics of corporate irresponsibility might turn their view around. Perhaps 'rights talk' is part of the problem. Doesn't an emphasis on individual rights invite people to think of 'number one': *me*, my rights, my freedoms, my interests?

A Kantian analysis rejects the shared premise. Companies cannot arise from private right (§2.2). We have already looked at this point historically (§4.1). Allow me to recapitulate the conceptual argument.

Artificial personhood creates a new bearer of legal rights and duties. For example, the company owns the factory – a property right. The company owes a debt to the bank – a contractual duty. The company must pay damages for negligence – a liability in civil law.

People make decisions which affect these assets and liabilities, in ways that can affect everyone's rightful situation. Directors act on behalf of the company; they govern employees who also act for the company; all of them can use corporate powers in ways that affect outsiders. But none of the participants own the factory. None of them own the company. None of them must pay company debts. With the caveat noted in §2.2.3, none of them are liable for damages.

Parallel points apply to shareholders (§4.1.3). They do not own the factory, or the company. They are not liable for company debts, or damages.

Contracts alter people's rights and duties *to one another*. However complex, contracts cannot alter the rights of people who do not take part in them (Ripstein 2016: 82 f). Contracting parties bind one another, equally. They may not bind outsiders.

Directors and shareholders gain powers to act for and through an artificial person: extra legal powers, with less legal responsibility. This bears on everyone's rightful situation, not just the supposedly contracting parties'. People can never achieve this by exercising their private rights. They exercise publicly authorised powers, civic rather than merely private (§1.3.3). These powers demand public justification.

4.2.4 A Kantian Framing of Corporate Social Responsibility, Business Regulation, and Shareholder Rights

In terms of *corporate social responsibility*, the Kantian point is this. Ethically, socially, and politically, we would like companies to act openly and above board, in ways that respect people and public goods. We would like directors and employees to take business ethics seriously. But are companies legally structured in ways that support virtuous and responsible conduct?

If companies and managers and markets often create socially undesirable consequences, the problem is not that people exercise their private rights, without properly considering their duties. The rights involved are not private.

Instead, another problem comes first. Public right grants rights and privileges to companies, and the people who act for them. But there are inadequate duties and safeguards to prevent social irresponsibility.

For debates about *business regulation*, a related point applies. Kant recognises the state's right and duty to impose rules for the sake of public well-being (6:325; §3.4.4). There may be good reasons to regulate business. But this is not the first issue, since the problem concerns *artificial* persons.

If those 'persons' tend to be indifferent or even hostile to public well-being, then we must reconsider the laws that create and structure their 'personality'. If companies often act irresponsibly, then reforms should address their characteristics, capacities, and propensities. Revising publicly granted powers does not 'interfere in' private rights or 'limit' private freedoms.

This point also bears on how we should frame regulations on companies and corporate markets. It is common to speak of regulations as 'red tape' that 'restricts' or 'interferes'. But corporate business is only possible through public right. When states regulate companies or corporate markets, it is misleading to see this as interference. Rather, law sets conditions on powers and privileges which it has itself created.

In discussions of *shareholder rights*, it is common to assume that shareholders own companies. Like other property-owners, they should have the right to use their property to their own advantage. For example, they may employ people to manage it in their interests (Friedman 1970). Such assumptions support the influential idea that company directors should pursue 'shareholder value'.

This story is based on a false premise. Shareholders do not own companies. Instead, they command a peculiar bundle of rights that could never arise from private right (§4.1.4). People and companies (§4.1.5) buy rights to govern an artificial person, that is, to elect its directors. There are no corresponding duties (with caveats: §4.0.1). Shareholders are not governed by those directors; they are not accountable for the company's actions or impacts. Financially, they may gain or lose, depending on whether the company does well, and the general mood of stock markets. But that is all.

Whatever may be said for or against this bundle, it can only arise from a political decision to authorise corporations with this governmental structure. Such decisions can never be 'perpetual' (§2.3): they cannot undercut the state's right to reform or citizens' duty to press for more rightful conditions. Like other sorts of corporation, companies must be structured and regulated in ways that are publicly justifiable.

4.3 The Purposes of Corporate Business

Section 2 argued that, on Kantian principles, a corporation must have a definite purpose (§2.4.2). This cannot be *merely* an individual or private end. The corporation must also have mechanisms to pursue this purpose intelligently and responsively. Section 3 set out a range of legitimate purposes. It also argued for the importance of public mechanisms to ensure that a corporation remains accountable to its purpose.

The early history of business corporations is not encouraging. We have seen Kant's blunt criticism of these colonial and military ventures (§4.1.1). The merchant-directors and shareholders were generally motivated by personal gain. That falls within their private right, even if we have ethical reservations. But it cannot merit state support. Indeed, the English Company was notorious for bribing politicians so that directors could retain their privileges (Robins 2012: 52 ff).

Modern legal frameworks are generally vague on companies' purpose. For example, the General Corporation Law of Delaware provides the basis for most

US business corporations. They can 'conduct or promote any lawful business or purposes' (§101).

That is just the same as for individual people: the law says that you should act within the law. Such an empty provision seems directly against the argument of Section 2. Individual people can already pursue 'lawful business and purposes'. Why grant them the powers and privileges involved in governing a distinct, artificial person?

4.3.1 Prosperity and Private Ends

I have noted one mistaken view of corporate purpose: a company exists in order to pursue shareholders' interests, since it is their property (§4.2.4). Still, many participants hope to become wealthy – whether by directing a business or by investing in stock markets. Profit-seeking is the most obvious factor which separates business companies from other types of corporation. Customers also seek better products and better value. Employees hope for well-paid, rewarding jobs. Let me suggest a Kantian way to recognise these common-sense points about people's private ends.

In 'Theory and Practice', Kant suggests that public right may support *prosperity*, understood as a *means towards more rightful conditions*:

> If the supreme power gives laws that are directed chiefly to happiness (the prosperity of the citizens, increased population and the like), this is not done as the end for which a civil constitution is established but merely as means for *securing a rightful condition* ... not in order, as it were, to make the people happy against its will but only to make it exist as a commonwealth. (T&P 8:298 f; see also Brosch 2024: Ch. 6)

This suggests two related arguments for states to authorise business corporations.

If companies contribute to prosperity, they may be useful *merely as means* to a rightful condition. Poverty and insecurity pit people against one another. They make it harder to care for public goods and engage in public reasoning. Vital social movements have been born out of deprivation, but their struggles have often been long and brutal. Every aspect of justice is harder when lives are pinched and hard.

There is also an obvious democratic argument. Prosperity is unlikely to go 'against [the people's] will'. This corresponds to the points about 'public opinion' and republicanism considered earlier (§3.1.2).

Either way, prosperity refers to a widely shared condition that supports right. Seen in this way, prosperity combines private ends and public purposes; it is an important *civic* goal (§1.3.3). Corporate markets may be a useful means to this.

4.3.2 Profit, Purpose, and Competition

Although profit is important, it cannot be the purpose of corporate business. To see why, we must make two distinctions.

First, I have stressed the difference between private ends and corporate purposes. The fact that people seek individual wealth, for example, does not make this the purpose of a business. It just explains why these people participate in the company.

Business competition introduces a second distinction. States chartered early business corporations as monopolies. (Thus the Dutch and English East India Companies.) Routine business incorporation works differently: it promotes competition, since anyone can create a new company. Additional laws ensure competition: laws against collusion and cartels; constraints on takeovers and mergers.

Of course, monopoly and cartel are good routes to safer, larger profits. Law rejects them. Competition undercuts profitability, at the same time as it forces companies to care about profitability: sustained losses spell corporate death – bankruptcy (§2.2.1), or perhaps takeover (Heath 2019). So we must distinguish corporate purposes (perhaps including profitability) from the broader purpose aimed at by companies law.

To survive and prosper in a competitive context, companies must do many things. They must produce and trade, satisfy buyers' wants and needs, look for unserved markets, employ workers, invest and innovate.

From different perspectives, it is possible to describe all these activities either as means or as ends. The company *must* do these things, at least to some minimal level, since they are necessary means for survival. Arguably, then, it does not make sense to lay them down as lawful purposes, let alone to create mechanisms for legal enforcement. (But see Mayer 2013 and 2022.)

At the same time, participants may see these activities as purposes. Directors and employees and companies may find a *sense of purpose* in them, beyond any individual gains. Decent employment, well-functioning products, reliable services, investments that look to the long-term yet permit innovation: all make important contributions to people's lives; all are worth doing well.

In well-structured markets, these activities contribute to prosperity and support rightful conditions. But these are larger goals, not purposes that corporate participants or companies could aim at. They can only be purposes from the point of view of public right, as the state lays down companies law and regulates corporate markets.

In turn, companies and the markets they participate in are means towards these ends, just as they are means towards people's private ends. That is also to say: profit is a purpose that individuals or companies may aim at. But it is not a purpose that public right should give weight to, except insofar as it contributes to prosperity and rightful conditions.

Let me underline the broader Kantian point. Artificial legal personality increases some people's legal powers to act and decreases their liabilities. This privilege should never function merely as a means for some people to satisfy their personal ends. It would be a direct attack on innate equality, if some people could bind others 'to more than [others] can in turn bind them' (6:237). It would betray public right, if people could use this power to practise social irresponsibility. To avoid these dangers, there must be public justifications and safeguards.

4.3.3 Public Justification

This account might suggest that the formal Kantian condition, corporate purpose, does not apply to businesses. Perhaps one aspect of Easterbrook and Fischel's view (§4.2.3) is correct: a company's 'purpose' is merely a compromise between various individual purposes and the activities these require. There are private ends: desires for goods and services, for pay and decent work, for a share in profits. There are necessary means: imperatives to produce and sell and innovate and invest and avoid losses. This provides a surprising rationale for the emptiness of companies law: to 'conduct or promote any lawful business or purposes' (§4.3).

Nonetheless, purpose still applies to the larger whole that arises when companies compete (Hussain 2023: 45 ff). This makes public reasoning more important – and more difficult. If we miss the role of public right in constituting these markets, it is easy to forget that there must be a rationale beyond people's private ends.

As an illustration, consider the case where these markets sharpen inequality, rather than creating shared prosperity. Shareholders gain; wealthy people who own many shares gain even more. Employees, especially lower-ranking ones, are paid a smaller share of business returns (§4.4.3; Anderson 2018).

One response is: this is just how markets work. Another response adds: therefore government needs to intervene, perhaps by taxation and redistributive policies. Then the counter-response: this interferes in private rights and limits private freedoms.

These responses assume that corporate markets are *not* created by government policies. But this is false: no corporation can exist without state authorisation. If corporate markets do not support rightful conditions, they fail on their own terms – that is, the terms of public right.

Regulations may be helpful – for example, minimum wage laws. They set conditions on corporate activity; they do not interfere in private rights. More fundamentally, however, the legal framework must be open to critique. I have pointed to three Kantian criteria.

First, corporations must not become a mere means for some people to extend their legal capacity to bind others, while insulating themselves from legal liability. This risk is built into the corporate form. It is more serious in the business context – partly because the ethos of personal gain is so entrenched, and partly because corporate purpose is harder to pin down here.

Second, from the point of view of public right, companies and corporate markets are a means to prosperity, understood as a means to support rightful conditions.

Third, these structures should limit risks of social irresponsibility. As well as 'policing' or regulation (§3.4.4), this means structuring companies and markets to support responsible conduct.

These are broad criteria that leave much space for judgement, both as to how things stand and as to how they might be improved. Towards the end of this section (§4.4.4), I will stress the importance of public information, if debates are to be meaningful and reforms to hit the mark.

4.4 Workers

Before modern Kantian business ethics, the *neo-Kantians* argued for 'ethical socialism'. Hermann Cohen (1904) and others advocated co-operative forms of economic activity, trade unionism, and socialist reforms (van der Linden 1988, Widmer 2024). They took inspiration from Kant's famous principle: we should not use people merely as means.

This idea finds echoes in Marx's famous criticism: capitalism makes *people out of things and things out of people* (1976: 209). Commodity fetishism treats things as if they have value in themselves; proletarians are treated as disposable commodities. 'Instrumentalisation' was an obvious way to interpret the exploitation that many contemporary workers suffered.

In most democratic countries, workers have since gained important rights, as I note in §4.4.2. Still, two Kantian concerns remain. First, organisations focused on financial returns are prone to exploit workers, especially lower-ranking ones. This is one way that employees may be used as mere means. Second, most employees cannot know whether they participate in corporate irresponsibility. They may be used as means to immoral ends.

4.4.1 Kant's Third Category of Acquired Right: Domestic or Status Right

After *property* and *contract*, Kant introduces a third form of acquired right: *domestic right* (§2.1). This concerns one person's '*status* in relation to' another (6:247, my emphasis). It includes the relation between servant and head of household.[8]

A status relation has a different form to the relation between contracting parties. There is a contract between master and servant. But to emphasise Kant's terminology: this contract adds *matter* (content such as rate of pay or working hours) to a distinct *form* of right.

This form, domestic or status right, is 'like rights to a thing'. The master is entitled to use the servant's active powers: 'I get a right to make arrangements about him' (6:259). Contracts are formally equal, but domestic right is not. One party *governs* the other.

As noted, Kant's account has major defects, to the point of contradicting innate equality (§2.4). Heads of household have coercive rights to 'fetch back' a servant who flees their post. Servants cannot be active citizens – they cannot vote, for example.

However, Kant's category has an important virtue. It gives legal form to authority relations (Castro 2014). The servant *belongs to* the household – not as a thing or a slave, but as a person who takes on duties towards the household. In this case, rights go both ways; so do duties. As Kant says, 'even the least of [a prince's] servants must have a coercive right against them' (T&P 8:294 n).

4.4.2 Employment as a Version of Status Right

Kant treats other types of employment as contractual (6:285). I suggest this is misleading, because it obscures the governmental aspect of employment. As with domestic service, contracts are important. But the underlying *form* is different (Williams 2024).

Modern legal systems recognise this. Lawyers refer to 'the employment contract' because its structure differs from contracts for goods or services. Unlike other contractors, employees have legal duties of *obedience and loyalty* (Deakin & Wilkinson 2005: 108).

Within a certain role, my employer determines how I use my time and active powers. They decide who I work with, control access to resources and information, specify duties and goals. Employment law requires me to perform these tasks (*obedience*) with attention to the employer's purposes (*loyalty*). In Kant's terms, I use my reason *privately* – to 'carry out another's commission' (8:38; §3.2.3).

The distinction between employee and contractor has resurfaced in the 'gig economy'. Uber drivers have taken legal action for recognition as employees, as

---

[8] I set aside Kant's other divisions – parent–child and husband–wife – since these raise issues beyond workplace authority. For an intersectional approach to employment based on Kant's categories, see Pascoe 2022.

opposed to contractors who sell their services. Since the corporation effectively subjects them to duties of loyalty and obedience, they should be granted the rights and protections of employees (Rosemain & Vidalon 2020).

This legal dispute reflects the other side of employment right: employers' duties. The authority relationship binds employees 'to more than [the employee] can in turn bind' the employer (to adapt Kant's language at 6:237). This formal inequality requires counterbalancing obligations. Paying a wage or salary is only one of these.

Like heads of households, employers bear legal liability for employees' actions. This is the legal doctrine of *respondeat superior*: 'the master answers' for his servant (Weinrib 2012: 185 ff). This transfer or sharing of liability cannot be decided as a matter of private right, since it affects the rights of third parties (§2.2.2).

More importantly, employers have duties of care. They govern employees' workplaces, so they must uphold health and safety. Likewise, freedom from bullying, harassment, and discrimination. To say employees should not be 'mere means' is also to acknowledge their lives beyond the workplace. Think of rights to holiday and sick leave, parental leave, minimum wages and periods of notice.

Employees also have limited rights to agency in the workplace. They are entitled to take part in trade unions – another type of corporation, structured to represent their interests. In a few jurisdictions, trade unions or worker representatives take part in workplace decisions (§4.0.1).

Of course, Kant could hardly foresee these rights. They were hard-won, not least through socialist and social democratic politics in which the neo-Kantians took a keen interest. They vary between jurisdictions; non-democratic countries often reject them. Still, the neo-Kantians drew on clear Kantian principles. Duties of obedience and loyalty correspond to the employer's authority, creating unequal powers to bind. This formal inequality is intolerable without formal counter-measures. (See Hussain 2023: 193 ff for a parallel Kantian argument.)

Artificial personhood adds a second dimension to this inequality. As large employers, corporations do not just give instructions and goals to individuals. They also govern workplaces: material conditions, authority relations, information flows, and procedures (Ciepley 2023). This second form of inequality allows much more intensive forms of government (Foucault 1977).

Kant's discussion of status right has many problems, and he could not anticipate modern employment. But his category forces us to recognise the essential problem. Law upholds a governmental relation. Innate equality demands that it be counterbalanced by other rights and duties.

4.4.3 Mere Means (i): Exploitation

Employees are means towards corporate ends. To judge whether they are *mere* means, we might ask some familiar questions: is their employment exploitative (rather than equitable), extorted (rather than voluntary), demeaning (rather than decent)? For simplicity, I have referred to all these problems as 'exploitation'. Philosophical and political discussions show how complex these issues are (e.g. Wood 2016). Here I just want to note two broad dangers.

First is the formal point already mentioned: when law sustains authority relations, it must ensure counterbalancing mechanisms (§4.4.2). If these are not well structured, then we should expect exploitation, at least for employees with fewer social advantages.

Second, the tougher financial pressures are, the more inclined corporations will be to take the shortcut: exploit workers. This applies to every type of corporation. Alongside the legal structure of shareholding, competition sharpens these pressures.

Although employees lack rights to participate in governing, they need not be powerless. They can bargain for better conditions – at least, if they are hard to replace or if they have an effective trade union. They can leave – if they can find another source of income. They can speak out about problems in the workplace – if they are not too afraid of dismissal or the other penalties that large organisations command. But those are big 'ifs'. None of them involve rights to participate in governing the business.

Kant's striking remark in the *Doctrine of Virtue* fits the case too well. Some people are 'favoured through the injustice of the government, which introduces an inequality of wealth that makes others need their beneficence' (6:454).

The injustice is not primarily to do with wealth. It concerns legally structured *powers to bind* – that is, to govern someone. In the sentence just quoted, Kant alludes to the miserable situation of needy people. They are subject to one sort of binding power. To live, they must submit to whatever conditions the wealthy place on their charity (Ripstein 2009: 272 ff).

The legal structures of shareholding and employment create another form of injustice. Wealthy people buy governmental power over companies. The company governs employees through legal duties of obedience and loyalty. Employees usually have no rights to take part in governing.

4.4.4 Mere Means (ii): Ethical Corruption

Here is a second issue, less often noted. Can employees know what they are means toward? – At the start of this Element, I noted how corporate employment can enable us act as 'useful members of the world' (6:446; §1.4). Decent employment allows us to act as means for others, but not *mere means*. We contribute to social goods; we gain income, opportunities, and social status. I have also noted the dangers of 'just following orders' (§1.1, §4.2.1) and corporate collaboration (§3.2.4, §3.4.3). Collective action is demanding; irresponsibility and incoherence are structural dangers.

The employment relation involves rights to use workers *without* granting them rights to participate in governing or to know anything beyond their immediate role (Anderson 2017). This creates hierarchy and discipline. It also makes it easier for people and organisations to ignore the effects of their conduct. Large organisations need deliberate mechanisms to gain knowledge of those impacts. But it is often easier and more profitable to ignore pollution or other externalities. It is certainly tempting to pretend all is well and to ignore signs that things are awry.

Every type of corporation offers examples of the resulting dangers: negligence and recklessness; abuse of participants or outsiders; petty privileges or grotesque gains for superiors; betrayals of legal purpose; organised cover for civil and criminal wrongs. Suspicions meet organisational indifference; allegations meet well-oiled denials.

But business corporations pose special risks. Some arise from the concerted production of goods and services. This requires intense material activity – fertile ground for adverse consequences. Some belong to their structure. I will stress one, concerning *knowledge*.

Legally, businesses' main obligation to gather information is financial: they must issue reports that reflect shareholders' interests. By contrast, employees have no rights to information. In fact, anyone with non-financial concerns faces greater uncertainty: not just employees, but even directors, not to mention customers and a wider public.

This creates moral vulnerability. Even if employees do not act directly against morality, they may still play a part in social irresponsibility. The risks are well-known – pollution and exploitation, short-termism and wilful blindness, and many more. Especially in competitive contexts, irresponsible shortcuts may spell the difference between viability and bankruptcy.

In general, knowledge only emerges after considerable harm. It needs public inquiries or investigative journalism or reports by officials overseeing bankruptcy. Too often, someone must blow the whistle; their life may be shattered before the full picture is clear.

This raises difficult issues about individual responsibility, consequences, and collective action. As we know, Kant's moral theory is not simply consequentialist. But he never advocates negligence or recklessness. Here I make only a minimal assumption: both people and organisations have responsibilities to *take care* concerning the consequences of their activity.[9]

Consider a corporation with a publicly declared purpose, open to public scrutiny and subject to public accountability. No one can know first-hand all that a large organisation is up to. But employees have reasonable grounds for trust – that they are means to worthwhile ends and *not* means towards damaging shortcuts. Without these safeguards, employees are means to they-cannot-know-what.

Kant's ideas in 'What Is Enlightenment?' (8:35 f) can illuminate the problem. An adult who has reached the 'age of majority' should take responsibility for their thought and conduct. But they can fall back into 'minority': a child-like stance of deference and ungrounded trust.

Minority is 'self-incurred' when adults 'lack the resolution and courage' to reason for themselves. By contrast, business employment *imposes* minority. Public right authorises companies without clear purposes. Reasoning and justification are harder than with other types of corporation. There are only limited mechanisms to check irresponsibility. We lack systematic ways to assess their impacts. Participants are often bound to secrecy and tempted to ignore risks and damage.

In the same essay, Kant argues that organisation requires 'a certain mechanism'. Employees must 'behave merely passively' and reason 'privately' (8:37; §3.2.3). Legal duties of obedience and loyalty reflect these ideas. They also reflect the basic practicalities: compromise is essential to every sort of collective action. Employees must often go along with actions or policies they think could be improved. In itself, this does not make them 'minors' or mere means.

However, Kant insists that the private use of reason must be compatible with its public use. Obedience and loyalty cannot mean duties to follow orders, in the dark as to wider activities and effects. Compromise should not tip into complicity. 'Passivity' and 'privacy' are tolerable, so long as they do not impose 'minority'. Active, public judgement must remain possible.

Without knowledge about companies' activities and impacts, employees act towards uncertain ends on uncertain terms, in the face of well-known risks of immorality and irresponsibility. It may not be clear who is to blame (§4.2.2). But the legal structure impairs moral agency. The 'humanity in [their] person' can become 'merely a means' (4:429).

---

[9] For discussion of negligence, see Ripstein (2016: Ch. 4) as well as my own account (2020). See also O'Neill's incisive remarks on the fundamental role of instrumental and consequential reasoning (2013a: 21 ff).

Conclusion to Section 4

Kant only saw the first stages of the business corporation. Applying his principles to modern business is not simple. The structure of Kant's 'metaphysics of morals' means we cannot expect easy guidance from the Categorical Imperative or his account of virtue. Instead, we must understand juridical structures, and expose them to critique. In addition, contemporary views differ sharply. Some extol companies' contributions to prosperity. Others deplore effects such as pollution, exploitation, and increasing inequality.

The hard truth is that both views have truth. Business corporations produce *and* pollute; trade *and* traffic; employ *and* exploit; innovate *and* externalise; compete *and* cut corners; support *and* undermine rightful conditions. In any given case, it is hard to know how far a company contributes to the prosperity that gives business a good name. It is hard to know how far it takes the time-honoured, shop-worn shortcuts that give business a bad name.

Although Kant offers no easy answers, his principles help explain these conflicting tendencies. Public reasoning often misses the essential role of public right in creating corporate markets. This makes it harder to understand and reform their legal structures.

One problem follows from the central argument of Section 2. Corporations should have a purpose and be accountable to it. Otherwise, they betray innate equality: they allow some people to exercise more legal powers with less liability; they empower some people to pursue private ends or to damage others' rights and interests.

This section has offered a limited defence of the absence of legally specified purpose. Competitive contexts require companies to do many things that may contribute to prosperity: for example, to serve customers, to innovate and invest, and to employ. But this is only a limited defence. It stands in tension with another aspect of the shareholder-based business corporation.

This dominant legal structure involves unequal rights to govern and partial duties to inform. People with spare wealth can buy governmental power over these businesses. By contrast, employees usually lack rights to participate in governing. Only shareholders have a legal right to information; this focuses only on their financial interests. As much as competitive businesses may contribute to prosperity, we know that they must be tempted to irresponsibility – such as pollution and exploitation, short-termism and wilful blindness.

This creates ethical problems for individuals: are corporate participants means towards prosperity or agents of irresponsibility? It also creates civic problems in public reasoning. There are many difficulties in recognising the legal structure; information is produced very selectively. We should not be surprised that public views differ sharply. But we may still be dismayed by how often public power seems helpless in the face of corporate irresponsibility.

5 Conclusion: Kant Incorporated

Kant offers a systematic basis for understanding corporations. Corporations combine public authority and private initiative to pursue important purposes, including the public use of reason, democratic participation, religious congregation, and charitable activity.

As such, corporations bridge the key distinctions of Kant's practical philosophy: right and ethics; public versus private right. Right is enriched when we look beyond individual freedoms and state authority, and understand how it can support shared contributions to civil society. Ethics is enriched when it compasses our responsibilities to sustain organisations that respect their participants and pursue worthwhile ends.

Incorporation is the basis of *all* the major organisations of modern societies. Long-term, collective activities require juridical form; many require 'a certain autonomy' from the state (7:17). While Kant could not foresee the variety of modern corporations, he saw some of the ways in which our societies depend on the social power, initiative and participation, and long-term planning that the corporate form enables.

Kant also clarified our modern common sense, no longer revolutionary: citizens should enjoy equal freedom. So his theory poses an essential challenge: how can corporate powers be compatible with this equality?

5.1 Autonomy and Heteronomy

Worthwhile corporations combine 'autonomy' and 'heteronomy' – for participants, and the corporation itself.

In different ways, participants are governed by the corporation – a sort of *heteronomy*, especially if we keep in mind how specific and intensive their duties may be. But participants often have some *autonomy*, too. Depending on the corporation's mode of government and their position within it, they may take part in governing or exercise initiative and judgement regarding their own contributions. They can also leave, although this may cost them dearly.

The corporation has 'a certain autonomy', too (7:17): it is not subject to the dictates of the state nor to the whims of private persons; it must be capable of intelligent, responsive activity. This is only possible if it can govern itself in the light of its animating purpose. Within that purpose and the wider limits of law, it is largely self-governing: a domain of power and activity at arm's length from the state.

This autonomy also enables corporations to help tackle the failings of other organisations, including the state. Political parties and well-functioning news media are essential to democracy (§3.1). Trade unions and civic organisations make vital contributions to more rightful conditions.

At the same time, a corporation is *heteronomous* in the sense that it must be governed by its purpose. A natural person can decide what to do with their lives – within the law; guided by unenforceable duties of virtue. That is what innate freedom *means*. By contrast, sovereign charters lay down specific purposes. Standing laws lay down a broad purpose that takes more definite shape for each corporation. When a charity is founded, for example, it specifies which 'public benefits' it will pursue.

This safeguard is vital: it would go against innate equality, if corporations or participants could act with the full freedom of private persons. They must abide by corporate purposes and policies. Kantian morality still applies, of course (§4.2.1). People are always moral agents and citizens before they are corporate participants. In the limit – for example, if corporations use people as mere means, or if a corporation betrays its purpose – participants may have to resign or raise concerns outside the corporation. In such cases, the juridical structure probably requires critique – not least, because it is likely to have corrupting effects on virtue, too (§3.3, §4.2.2).

5.2 Between Public and Private

In the Introduction, I set out two versions of the public-private distinction in Kant (§1.3.3). In an abstract sense, all right is private in a state of nature; all right is public in a public legal order. Since we usually move within a legal order, another contrast is more familiar. Private persons exercise private rights and duties; public right names the prerogatives of states and their officials. This distinction gives rise to a third category, since 'private citizens' may exercise public responsibilities – by voting, for example, or reasoning publicly. I have referred to these as civic rights.

In a celebrated discussion, David Ciepley placed corporations 'beyond public and private' (2013). In the same spirit, I have argued that corporations involve both public and private elements, given the combination of rights and duties they involve. Since artificial persons cannot arise from private right, they must be authorised by public right. Since these 'persons' have no living body, natural persons must act for them.

In essence, people lend their active powers to the corporation. They give time and energy, skills and knowledge, commitment and initiative: all matters of innate right. A range of legal relations allows this. Officers, directors, or trustees have powers to act for the corporation. Members and employees take part in different ways. Alongside enabling laws, a charter or governing document spells out their powers to govern and participate, as well as the corporation's purpose.

The result is a huge diversity of corporations. Some are small and relevant only to a few people. Others are huge and complex, of wide significance across generations. We might say that there is a continuum. Some corporations are 'private', for most intents and purposes: a local sports club or a small religious group, for example. Some are 'civic': major charities and trusts, for instance. Others are better termed 'public': a state university or a political party, say. However, the many meanings of public and private create room for disagreement, especially when we come to business corporations.

This Element has argued that Kantians should insist on one aspect. Artificial persons can only exist and act if people have powers to act for them. The powers involved go beyond those of private right. Only the state can grant these powers. It must be cautious in doing so, because innate equality is on the line.

Of course, people use corporations to pursue ends that they care about – be it sporting participation or religious congregation, academic research or political power, or simply the personal rewards that participation can bring. Indeed, people *must* have their own reasons for participating. Corporate participation may not be coerced or compulsory. People should never be mere means to corporate purposes, or to the ends of other participants.

At the same time, the extra power of artificial personhood must not be a *mere* means for people to pursue their personal ends, however harmless or worthwhile those might be. The powers involved bear on *everyone's* legal standing; they require public justification and public safeguards. In this regard, all corporate activity lies *between* public and private.

5.3 Justification and Knowledge

A Kantian perspective justifies many different types of corporation. It also rejects others: above all, feudal orders that entrench privilege. Fortunately, those corporations are largely history.

But the corporate form itself holds dangers, alongside its undoubted benefits for long-term cooperation. I have stressed its inherent tension with innate equality, as well as problems of power, information, and responsibility. These problems are especially serious in the business context, not least because debates often miss how business corporations depend on the grant of public power.

Given these problems, it is not enough for law to authorise corporations on the basis of worthwhile purposes, such as 'public benefit' or religious congregation. It is not enough for a corporation to state the specific benefits or purposes it aims at. In the business case, we cannot simply trust that competitive contexts will foster contributions to prosperity.

There must be mechanisms to ensure that these purposes are realised. This requires corporate government that is intelligent, accountable, and open to reform and improvement. It requires ways to know if purposes are achieved, and if there are other effects or externalities.

This is hard, because corporations dilute responsibility. Formally, people act on behalf of an artificial person: they do not bear the full liabilities of someone who acts in their own name; they act together with others. Materially, they may have access to powers and resources that no private individual could ever have.

Alongside the formal tension with innate equality, these facts create enormous scope for unintended effects and wilful blindness, not to mention outright deception and fraud. Section 4 argued that business provides the most striking illustration. But no type of corporation is immune from these dangers.

All corporations depend on public authority to exist and to act – businesses no less than charities or universities or political parties. That power must be justified. We must be able to reason publicly about them; meaningful debate is only possible if we know what they are doing and causing. It must be possible to reform when they fall short. Morality and freedom demand nothing less.

Kantian Texts and Abbreviations

Quotations rely on translations in the Cambridge Edition of Kant's works, with some amendments. Kant's texts are referenced by **<volume number>:<page number>** in the standard Academy edition of his works. The relevant volumes are:

4:   *Groundwork of the Metaphysics of Morals* (1785)
5:   *Critique of Practical Reason* (1788)
6:   *Metaphysics of Morals* (1797) or *Religion* (1793) – if the latter, I say so
7:   *Conflict of the Faculties* (1798)
8:   'What Is Enlightenment?' (1784), 'Theory and Practice', or *Towards Perpetual Peace* – I use the abbreviations below to indicate the last two

Abbreviations for Kant's Works

Feyerabend   Natural right course lecture notes by Feyerabend (1784)
Groundwork   *Groundwork of the Metaphysics of Morals* (1785)
PP   *Towards Perpetual Peace* (1795)
Religion   *Religion Within the Boundaries of Mere Reason* (1793)
T&P   'Theory and Practice', or in full: 'On the common saying: That may be correct in theory, but it is of no use in practice' (1793)

References

Anderson, E. 2017. *Private Government: How Employers Rule Our Lives (and Why We Don't Talk about It)*. Princeton: Princeton University Press.

Anderson, E. 2018. The great reversal: How neoliberalism turned the economic aspirations of classical liberalism upside down in favour of capital interests. *IPPR Progressive Review* 25(2): 202–213.

Arnoldt, D. H. 1746. *Ausführliche und mit Urkunden versehene Historie der Königsbergischen Universität*. Band I. Königsberg in Preußen: Johann Heinrich Hartung.

Barker, E. 1959. *From Alexander to Constantine: Passages and Documents Illustrating the History of Social and Political Ideas 336BC–AD337*. Oxford: Clarendon Press.

Blackstone, W. 1765. *Commentaries on the Laws of England, Book the First*. Oxford: Clarendon Press. https://avalon.law.yale.edu/subject_menus/blackstone.asp.

Boix, C. 2007. The emergence of parties and party systems. In C. Boix & S. C. Stokes, eds., *The Oxford Handbook of Comparative Politics*. Oxford: Oxford University Press, 499–521.

Bouterwek, F. 2014 [1797]. Review of Kant, *Metaphysical Foundations of the Doctrine of Right*. Trans. Kenneth Westphal. *Kant Studies Online*: https://kantstudiesonline.net/uploads/files/BouterwekWestphal02214.pdf.

Bowie, N. E. 2017. *Business Ethics: A Kantian Perspective* (2nd ed.). New York: Cambridge University Press.

Brosch, A. 2024. *Haus, Markt, Staat: Ökonomie in Kants praktischer Philosophie und Anthropologie*. Berlin: De Gruyter.

Bundeskunsthalle. 2023. *Kritische Interventionen in der Ausstellung: Immanuel Kant und die offenen Fragen – DFG Koselleck Projekt "Wie umgehen mit . . . ?"* https://wieumgehenmitrsa.uni-jena.de/kritische-interventionen-zu-kant-und-die-offenen-fragen/.

Capps, P. & Rivers, J. 2024. *The Postulate of Public Right*. Cambridge: Cambridge University Press.

Castro, S. 2014. The morality of unequal autonomy: Reviving Kant's concept of status for stakeholders. *Journal of Business Ethics* 121(4): 593–606.

Ciepley, D. 2013. Beyond public and private: Toward a political theory of the corporation. *American Political Science Review* 107(1): 139–158.

Ciepley, D. 2017. Is the US government a corporation? The corporate origins of modern constitutionalism. *American Political Science Review* 111(2): 418–435.

Ciepley, D. 2023. The corporation as a chartered government. *Hofstra Law Review* 51(4): 815–877.

Coffee Jr, J. C. 1981. 'No soul to damn: No body to kick': An unscandalized inquiry into the problem of corporate punishment. *Michigan Law Review* 79(3): 386–459.

Cohen, H. 1904. *Ethik des reinen Willens (System der Philosophie, zweiter Teil)*. Berlin: Bruno Cassirer.

Cordelli, C. 2020. *The Privatized State*. Princeton: Princeton University Press.

Cornuelle, R. 1991 (5 April). New work for invisible hands. *Times Literary Supplement* 4592: 5–6.

Deakin, S. F. & Wilkinson, F. 2005. *The Law of the Labour Market: Industrialization, Employment, and Legal Evolution*. Oxford: Oxford University Press.

Doyle, W. 2019. *The French Revolution: A Very Short Introduction* (2nd ed.). Oxford: Oxford University Press.

Easterbrook, F. H. & Fischel, D. R. 1989. The corporate contract. *Columbia Law Review* 89: 1416–1448.

Euler, W. L. & Stiening, G. 1995. '... und nie der Pluralität Widersprach'? Zur Bedeutung von Immanuel Kants Amtsgeschäften. *Kant-Studien* 86(1): 54–69.

Foucault, M. 1977. *Discipline and Punish: The Birth of the Prison*. Trans. Alan Sheridan. Harmondsworth: Penguin.

Friedman, M. 1970 (September 13). The social responsibility of business is to increase its profits. *New York Times Magazine* (variously reprinted).

Gelderblom, O., de Jong, A., & Jonker, J. 2013. The formative years of the modern corporation: The Dutch East India Company VOC, 1602–1623. *Journal of Economic History* 73(4): 1050–1076.

Gradenwitz, O. 1904. Der Wille des Stifters. In Universität Königsberg, ed., *Zur Erinnerung an Immanuel Kant: Abhandlungen aus Anlass der hundertsten Wiederkehr des Tages seines Todes*. Halle a.S.: Verlag der Buchhandlung des Waisenhauses, 180–202.

Harris, R. 2000. *Industrializing English Law: Entrepreneurship and Business Organization, 1720–1844*. Cambridge: Cambridge University Press.

Heath, J. 2019. The moral status of profit. In M. D. White, ed., *The Oxford Handbook of Ethics and Economics*. Oxford: Oxford University Press, 337–357.

Heffernan, M. 2011. *Wilful Blindness: Why We Ignore the Obvious at Our Peril*. Toronto: Doubleday Canada.

Herzog, L. 2018. *Reclaiming the System: Moral Responsibility, Divided Labour, and the Role of Organizations in Society*. Oxford: Oxford University Press.

Hochstrasser, T. J. 2000. *Natural Law Theories in the Early Enlightenment*. Cambridge: Cambridge University Press.

Hussain, W. 2023. *Living with the Invisible Hand: Markets, Corporations, and Human Freedom* (eds. A. Ripstein & N. Vrousalis). New York: Oxford University Press.

Klein, J. T. 2015. Freedom of the press: A Kantian approach. *Estudos Kantianos* 3(1): 83–92.

Kleingeld, P. 2018. Moral autonomy as political analogy: Self-legislation in Kant's *Groundwork* and the *Feyerabend Lectures on Natural Law* (1784). In S. Bacin & O. Sensen, eds., *The Emergence of Autonomy in Kant's Moral Philosophy*. Cambridge: Cambridge University Press, 158–175.

Kleingeld, P. 2025. Independence and Kant's positive conception of freedom. In M. Brecher & P.-A. Hirsch, eds., *Law and Morality in Kant*. Cambridge: Cambridge University Press, 262–284.

Klikauer, T. 2016. *Hegel's Moral Corporation*. New York: Palgrave Macmillan.

Kraakman, R., Armour, J., Davies, P. et al. 2017. *The Anatomy of Corporate Law: A Comparative and Functional Approach* (3rd ed.). Oxford: Oxford University Press.

Kuehn, M. 2001. *Kant: A Biography*. Cambridge: Cambridge University Press.

Kurki, V. A. J. 2023. *Legal Personhood*. Cambridge: Cambridge University Press.

Levy, J. 2014. *Rationalism, Pluralism, and Freedom*. Oxford: Oxford University Press.

Maliks, R. 2022. *Kant and the French Revolution*. Cambridge: Cambridge University Press.

Marx, K. 1867/1976. *Capital: A Critique of Political Economy, Volume One*. Trans. Ben Fowkes. Harmondsworth: Penguin.

Mayer, C. 2013. *Firm Commitment: Why the Corporation Is Failing Us and How to Restore Trust in It*. Oxford: Oxford University Press.

Mayer, C. 2022. What is wrong with corporate law? The purpose of law and the law of purpose. *Annual Review of Law and Social Science* 18: 283–296.

Moran, K. 2021. Kant on traveling blacksmiths and passive citizenship. *Kant-Studien* 112(1): 105–126.

Muthu, S. 2008. Adam Smith's critique of international trading companies: Theorizing 'globalization' in the Age of Enlightenment. *Political Theory* 36(2): 185–212.

National Co-operative Archive. 2014. *Acting on Principle: How Co-operatives Became Legal*. www.archive.coop/hive/acting-on-principle.

O'Neill, O. 1984. Paternalism and partial autonomy. *Journal of Medical Ethics* 10(4): 173–178.

O'Neill, O. 1985. Between consenting adults. *Philosophy & Public Affairs* 14(3): 252–277.

O'Neill, O. 2013a. *Acting on Principle: An Essay on Kantian Ethics* (2nd ed.). Cambridge: Cambridge University Press.

O'Neill, O. 2013b. The rights of journalism and the needs of audiences. *King's Review*. www.kingsreview.co.uk/essays/the-rights-of-journalism-and-the-needs-of-audiences.

Pascoe, J. 2022. *Kant's Theory of Labour*. Cambridge: Cambridge University Press.

Paton, G. W. 1972. *A Textbook of Jurisprudence* (4th ed., eds. G. W. Paton & D. P. Derham). Oxford: Oxford University Press.

Pistor, K., Keinan, Y., Kleinheisterkamp, J., & West, M. D. 2002. Evolution of corporate law: A cross-country comparison. *University of Pennsylvania Journal of International Economic Law* 23(4): 791–871.

Preiss, J. 2014. Global labor justice and the limits of economic analysis. *Business Ethics Quarterly* 24(1): 55–83.

Ripstein, A. 2009. *Force and Freedom: Kant's Legal and Political Philosophy*. Cambridge, MA: Harvard University Press.

Ripstein, A. 2010. Kantian legal philosophy. In D. Patterson, ed., *A Companion to Philosophy of Law and Legal Theory* (2nd ed.). Chichester: Wiley-Blackwell, 392–405.

Ripstein, A. 2016. *Private Wrongs*. Cambridge, MA: Harvard University Press.

Robins, N. 2012. *The Corporation that Changed the World: How the East India Company Shaped the Modern Multinational* (2nd ed.). London: Pluto Press.

Rosemain, M. & Vidalon, D. 2020 (4 March). Top French court deals blow to Uber by giving driver 'employee' status. *Reuters*. www.reuters.com/article/idUSKBN20R23E/.

Shaw, J. 1887. *Charters Relating to the East India Company from 1600 to 1761: Reprinted from a Former Collection with Some Additions and a Preface for the Government of Madras*. Madras: R. Hill at the Government Press.

Stewart, H. 2014. Kantian police: Limits on consent in regulatory law. *New Criminal Law Review* 17(1): 1–22.

Strachwitz, Rupert. 2010. *Die Stiftung – ein Paradox?* Stuttgart: Lucius & Lucius.

Thieme, H. 1960. Statistische Materialien zur Konzessionierung von Aktiengesellschaften in Preussen bis 1867. *Jahrbuch für Wirtschaftsgeschichte / Economic History Yearbook* 1: 285–300.

Timmermann, J. 2024. The quandary of infanticide in Kant's 'Doctrine of Right'. *Archiv für Geschichte der Philosophie* 106(2): 267–294.

van der Linden, H. 1988. *Kantian Ethics and Socialism*. Indianapolis: Hackett.

Van de Vijver, A. 2022. Morality of lobbying for tax benefits: A Kantian perspective. *Journal of Business Ethics* 181(1): 57–68.

Varden, H. 2020. *Sex, Love, and Gender: A Kantian Theory*. Oxford: Oxford University Press.

Vrousalis, N. 2022. Interdependent independence: Civil self-sufficiency and productive community in Kant's theory of citizenship. *Kantian Review* 27(3): 443–460.

Weinrib, E. J. 2012. *The Idea of Private Law* (revised edition). Oxford: Oxford University Press.

White, M. 2011. *Kantian Ethics and Economics: Autonomy, Dignity, and Character*. Stanford: Stanford University Press.

Widmer, E. 2024. *Left-Kantianism in the Marburg School*. Berlin: De Gruyter.

Williams, B. 1985. *Ethics and the Limits of Philosophy*. London: Fontana.

Williams, G. 2020. Taking responsibility for negligence and non-negligence. *Criminal Law and Philosophy* 14(1): 113–134.

Williams, G. 2024. Employment, status, hierarchy: On Jordan Pascoe, *Kant's Theory of Labour*. *Con-Textos Kantianos* 20: 7–15.

Wood, A. 2016. Unjust exploitation. *Southern Journal of Philosophy* 54(S1): 92–108.

Legal References: Charters, Statutes, and Cases.

(See also Arnoldt 1746, Barker 1959, and Shaw 1887, above.)

Charter, Statutes and Ordinances of the University of Lancaster. 1964/2018. www.lancaster.ac.uk/strategic-planning-and-governance/governance/.

General Corporation Law of the State of Delaware. N.d. https://delcode.delaware.gov/title8/Title8.pdf.

Octrooi verleend aan de Verenigde Oostindische Compagnie (VOC) in 1602 [agreement for the Dutch East India Company, 1602]. www.vocsite.nl/geschiedenis/octrooi1602/.

Trustees of Dartmouth College v. Woodward. 1819. *United States Reports* 17: 518–715.

Acknowledgements

For comments on versions of this Element, I am very grateful to: Lucy Allais, Carla Bagnoli, Lisa Herzog, Pauline Kleingeld, Katharina Kraus, Thomas Mertens, Corinna Mieth, Sofie Møller, Jason Neyers, Jordan Pascoe, Arthur Ripstein, Oliver Sensen, Tijn Smits, Martin Sticker, Helga Varden, Jan Willem Wieland, and Ewa Wyrębska. Special thanks to Martin for tea supplies and Lucy for extra input on Section 4!

Many thanks to the following people for organising events at which I've presented some of these ideas, as well as to audiences at these: Sorin Baiasu and Howard Williams (ECPR Hamburg, 2018), Matthias Hoesch and Martin Sticker (Münster, 2018), Rutger Claassen and Philipp Stehr (Utrecht, 2021), Paula Satne (Leeds, 2024), Larissa Berger, Elke Schmidt, and Dieter Schönecker (Bonn, 2024).

For additional discussions and input, I would like to thank: Joel Anderson, Sorin Baiasu, Eric Boot, Martin Brecher, Max Brennan, Ruth Chadwick, Jan Clarke (The Burn), David Ciepley, Richard Endörfer, Andrea Esser, Katrin Flikschuh, Oscar Gelderblom, Philipp-Alexander Hirsch, Sarah Holtman, Morris Kaplan, Kasim Khorasanee, Conrad Krausche, Chris Macleod, Chris May, Marion McClintock, Kate Moran, Steve Naragon, Johannes Nickl, Onora O'Neill, Alice Pinheiro Walla, Felix Pinkert, Joe Saunders, Alison Stone, Jens Timmermann, Sebastiaan Tijsterman, and Kenneth Westphal. I owe a further debt of gratitude to two reviewers for exceptionally constructive input, as well as to the editors of this series.

For personal and professional support, I would like to record my deep gratitude to Robert Geyer and Chris Macleod, as Heads of my Department at Lancaster University. Many thanks, too, to Mari Mikkola, as Head of Philosophy at the University of Amsterdam, who enabled a very happy research stay there.

For research funding, I am very grateful to the UK Arts and Humanities Research Council (grant number AH/X002365/1) and the Deutsche Forschungsgemeinschaft (project number 508354046), as well as to my project collaborators, Corinna Mieth, Martin Sticker and Ewa Wyrębska (https://sites.google.com/view/usingpeoplewell).

Dedication

This Element is for my parents, David and Verolys Williams.

Cambridge Elements

The Philosophy of Immanuel Kant

Desmond Hogan
Princeton University

Desmond Hogan joined the philosophy department at Princeton in 2004. His interests include Kant, Leibniz and German rationalism, early modern philosophy, and questions about causation and freedom. Recent work includes 'Kant on the Foreknowledge of Contingent Truths', *Res Philosophica* 91(1) (2014); 'Kant's Theory of Divine and Secondary Causation', in Brandon Look (ed.) *Leibniz and Kant*, Oxford University Press (2021); 'Kant and the Character of Mathematical Inference', in Carl Posy and Ofra Rechter (eds.) *Kant's Philosophy of Mathematics Vol. I*, Cambridge University Press (2020).

Howard Williams
University of Cardiff

Howard Williams was appointed Honorary Distinguished Professor at the Department of Politics and International Relations, University of Cardiff in 2014. He is also Emeritus Professor in Political Theory at the Department of International Politics, Aberystwyth University, a member of the Coleg Cymraeg Cenedlaethol (Welsh-language national college) and a Fellow of the Learned Society of Wales. He is the author of *Marx* (1980); *Kant's Political Philosophy* (1983); *Concepts of Ideology* (1988); *Hegel, Heraclitus and Marx's Dialectic* (1989); *International Relations in Political Theory* (1992); *International Relations and the Limits of Political Theory* (1996); *Kant's Critique of Hobbes: Sovereignty and Cosmopolitanism* (2003); *Kant and the End of War* (2012) and is currently editor of the journal Kantian Review. He is writing a book on the Kantian legacy in political philosophy for a new series edited by Paul Guyer.

Allen Wood
Indiana University

Allen Wood is Ward W. and Priscilla B. Woods Professor Emeritus at Stanford University. He was a John S. Guggenheim Fellow at the Free University in Berlin, a National Endowment for the Humanities Fellow at the University of Bonn and Isaiah Berlin Visiting Professor at the University of Oxford. He is on the editorial board of eight philosophy journals, five book series and The Stanford Encyclopedia of Philosophy. Along with Paul Guyer, Professor Wood is co-editor of The Cambridge Edition of the Works of Immanuel Kant and translator of the Critique of Pure Reason. He is the author or editor of a number of other works, mainly on Kant, Hegel and Karl Marx. His most recently published books are *Fichte's Ethical Thought*, Oxford University Press (2016) and *Kant and Religion*, Cambridge University Press (2020). Wood is a member of the American Academy of Arts and Sciences.

About the Series

This Cambridge Elements series provides an extensive overview of Kant's philosophy and its impact upon philosophy and philosophers. Distinguished Kant specialists provide an up-to-date summary of the results of current research in their fields and give their own take on what they believe are the most significant debates influencing research, drawing original conclusions.

Cambridge Elements

The Philosophy of Immanuel Kant

Elements in the Series

Kant on Freedom
Owen Ware

Kant on Self-Control
Marijana Vujošević

Kant on Rational Sympathy
Benjamin Vilhauer

The Moral Foundation of Right
Paul Guyer

The Postulate of Public Right
Patrick Capps and Julian Rivers

Kant on the History and Development of Practical Reason
Olga Lenczewska

Kant's Ideas of Reason
Katharina T. Kraus

Kant on Marriage
Charlotte Sabourin

Kant and Teleology
Thomas Teufel

Kant on Social Suffering
Nuria Sánchez Madrid

Kant's Natural Philosophy
Marius Stan

Kant Incorporated
Garrath Williams

A full series listing is available at: www.cambridge.org/EPIK

For EU product safety concerns, contact us at Calle de José Abascal, 56–1°, 28003 Madrid, Spain or eugpsr@cambridge.org.

www.ingramcontent.com/pod-product-compliance
Lightning Source LLC
LaVergne TN
LVHW011852060526
838200LV00054B/4295